2 ⁰⁰

D1524590

Mrs. Ma's Chinese Cookbook

MRS. MA'S
CHINESE COOKBOOK
by Nancy Chih Ma

CHARLES E. TUTTLE COMPANY: PUBLISHERS
Rutland, Vermont and Tokyo, Japan

Representatives

For Continental Europe:
BOXERBOOKS, INC., ZURICH

For the British Isles:
PRENTICE-HALL INTERNATIONAL. INC.. London

For Canada:
HURTIG PUBLISHERS, Edmonton

For Australasia:
BOOK WISE (AUSTRALIA) PTY. LTD.
104-108 Sussex Street, Sydney

Published by the
Charles E. Tuttle Company, Inc.
of Rutland, Vermont & Tokyo, Japan
with editorial offices at
Suido 1-chome, 2-6, Bunkyo-ku, Tokyo

Library of Congress
Catalog Card No. 60-12197

International Standard Book
No. 0-8048-0410-9

First printing, 1960
Thirty-third printing, 1977

Printed in Japan

TABLE OF CONTENTS

5

Table of Contents

7

Table of
Contents

9

FORE-WORD

There is an old Chinese saying: "When you prepare a dish, you must keep three things in mind: it must be pleasing to the eye, the aroma must be appealing, and it must be appetizing." For this reason, you can expect that each Chinese dish, whether the most economical or the most elaborate, will always be colorful, have a delightful aroma, and taste delicious.

Because I was born in a Manchurian banker's family, I never had the opportunity to prepare even one single Chinese dish while I was in China. It was only after my arrival in Japan that I became very enthusiastic about learning how to prepare Chinese dishes. I returned to Hong Kong several times, and during those sojourns I studied every phase of Chinese cooking. I was surprised and delighted to discover at that time that Chinese food was not only easy to prepare but economical as well.

In 1953 I was asked by the editor of one of Japan's foremost women's magazines, *Fujin no Tomo,* to submit a few Chinese recipes for the benefit of the readers. This led to the publication, in 1957, of my Chinese cookbook in Japanese, *Chugoku no Katei Ryori,* which was brought out under the auspices of this magazine. And the publication of my book led, in turn, to other interesting associations.

One result was that the mothers of the Parent-Teacher Association of the American School in Japan, which my children attend, asked me to give them lessons in Chinese cooking. Shortly after this, I was invited by Mrs. Fox, wife of Professor Guy Fox, of Michigan State University, to hold a class for the wives of Fulbright scholars in Japan. I was next honored with a request that I conduct classes for members of the Japanese Imperial Family, among whom were Princess Higashikuni, Princess Fushimi, Princess Kaya, Princess Ri, Princess Takeda, and others. Then came an invitation to instruct some of the teachers at the American School. Through these associations I was able to share my enthusiasm for the art of Chinese cooking with my friends from many parts of the world.

It was at the suggestion of one of the teachers at the American School that I began to work on an English translation of the cookbook that I had published in Japanese. I was extremely pleased at the great interest shown in my recipes and delighted to find a means of putting them before a wider public. I should therefore like to take advantage of this opportunity to thank all those friends who have encouraged me in my venture. I should also like to express my particular appreciation to the photographers Mr. Y. Saeki and Mr. H. Kakizaki, who provided, respectively, the colored and the black-and-white illustrations for the book.

Because I believe sincerely in the old Chinese proverb that says: "Good food brings happiness," I hope that you will have many enjoyable hours and much pleasure from the delicious dishes that this book will teach you how to prepare. I hope, too, that through the exchange of cooking experiences we may help to bring about closer friendship among the people of this world.

1960   NANCY CHIH MA

THE CHINESE CUISINE

TABLE SETTING AND ENTERTAINMENT. Although there is no objection to using Western-style tableware for the serving of Chinese food, the atmosphere of a Chinese dinner is naturally enhanced by the use of typical Chinese dishes and utensils. For this reason, beautifully colored, though not necessarily expensive, porcelain and china are frequently used.

Each set consists of a bowl for rice, a bowl for soup, a dish for the main courses, a small dish for sauce or condiments, a dessert dish, a wine cup, a porcelain soup spoon, and a pair of chopsticks. All the ingredients to be used in Chinese dishes are cut into convenient sizes in the kitchen before serving, so that no carving instruments are required at the table.

It goes without saying that dishes attractively arranged to please the eye serve as a stimulus to the appetite when they are filled with flavorful food. In contrast to the round shape of many Chinese dinner tables, dishes are often placed in a square, with a bowl for soup in the middle.

At the dinner table, the guest of honor is seated opposite the door, with the host or hostess across from him. When the first main dish is served, the host will propose a toast to his guests by saying: "Kan pei," which is the equivalent of the American toast, "Bottoms up." At this time, the guests should express their appreciation to their host for his hospitality.

The dinner begins with three or four cold dishes served separately or on a Lazy Susan type of platter as hors d'œuvres. These appetizers are placed on the table before the guests are seated. Four hot fried or sautéed dishes will then be served, and four steamed or braised dishes will follow, along with the rice. If the dinner is informal, it will usually consist of only four dishes and one soup. For an Oriental atmosphere, the soup should be served according to Chinese custom after all of the entrées have been offered, but before the dessert.

RICE AND ITS PREPARATION. Rice is the staple food of southern China. In the northern provinces, wheat and other grains are preferred. The water buffalo is a great asset in the preparation of the land, but the planting, reaping, and threshing are still done by human hands. In southern China, women also work in the fields.

Rice is planted in water paddies. As the plants grow, the water is hidden by the graceful blades of the leaves, and the fields take on a luxuriant appearance. When the wind ripples the fields of rice into waves of green, the sight is a beautiful one to see.

The rice harvest today is as colorful and primitive as it was in ancient days. Harvest time is a happy time among the farmers, and the threshing season is a busy one for them. As we eat rice, we always think of the old Chinese proverb: "Each single grain contains a farmer's hard work."

When you prepare rice, wash it several times until the water runs clear. Use one cup of rice to one and a half cups of water for "dry" rice and one cup of rice to two cups of water for soft rice. Boil the rice over a high flame until most of the water is absorbed. Then turn the flame low and simmer the rice for 20 minutes more, leaving the cover on. One cup of uncooked rice makes two cups of cooked rice. Insufficient water makes the rice hard. Cooked rice will keep for one week in the refrigerator and can be used for fried rice.

TEA. Generally, all classes of people in China drink tea. The habit is one of very long standing. In Peking, especially in the spring, when the wind blows strongly out of Mongolia and the rains seldom come, the human body feels "dry." Enticing street tea stands are scattered everywhere. As a welcome, the Chinese always offer a cup of tea to a guest.

The varieties of Chinese tea are numerous. Wu I Cha, Yang Shen Cha, Lung Cha, Mo Li Cha, and Hsiang Pien are only a few of the well-known green teas. Kee Mun, Liu An, Wu Long, and Pekoe are the better-known black teas. Jasmine tea, with its delightful scent, is also quite popular.

To prepare tea, put one teaspoonful of tea leaves into a Chinese teacup. Pour boiling water over the tea leaves and replace the lid. In three minutes the tasty tea will be ready. Partially remove the lid and drink through the opening. The lid will keep the tea leaves inside. Sugar and milk are never used. Instead of brewing the tea in individual cups, you may use a teapot.

WINE: Chinese wine is usually made from rice, but in some cases from other grains. It serves to give added flavor to either hot or cold Chinese food. Some of the best wines, being quite old, go well with both fish and meat.

Shao Hsing is the most popular wine in China. According to old custom, whenever a baby girl is born, the parents must bury a number of jars of Shao Hsing, storing them until the girl is to be married. Thus, on her wedding day, they will be assured the enjoyment of a delicious wine with their guests.

Glutinous rice is the source of Shao Hsing, and the wine should be at least one year old. After it has aged for five years or more, it is known as Hua Tiao (flower decoration) after the floral pattern of the jars in which it is kept.

Among Western wines and liqueurs, sherry, brandy, or cognac may be substituted in recipes that call for Chinese wine. Japanese saké is also an excellent substitute.

SIZES AND AMOUNTS OF INGREDIENTS. Since the ingredients called for in this book are those commonly used in the Orient, they differ occasionally from those known in the West. Almost all of them, however, can be obtained without difficulty, and the more exotic-sounding items are available at Chinese and Japanese food stores and restaurants. In cases where suitable substitutions can be made, these are suggested in the recipes. The sizes of typical ingredients can best be judged from the photograph on page 16. The following general suggestions will be helpful:

Abalone, canned: Size of can is No. 2.

Bamboo shoot: If fresh, peel and boil for 20 minutes. If canned, boiling is not required, but white calcium deposit should be scraped out before bamboo is used.

Bean curd: Soft, white, custard-like paste made from soy beans. It is called *tou fu* in Chinese, *tōfu* in Japanese. One cake equals two cups or three-quarters of a pound. It spoils quickly in warm climates.

Bean sprouts: Sprouts of green beans, called *tou ya ts'ai* in Chinese, *moyashi* in Japanese. Heads and tails should be removed before sprouts are used. Canned bean sprouts should be drained before using.

Chinese cabbage: Celery cabbage.

Cucumbers: Oriental cucumbers are only about one-third the size of the American variety when full-grown.

Eggplants: Oriental eggplants are much smaller than the Western variety and are about the size of a large pear.

Flour: Wheat flour is meant unless otherwise specified.

Green peppers: Full-grown Oriental green peppers are ordinarily smaller in size than the American variety.

Ham: Boiled ham, approximately four inches in diameter.

Mushrooms: Dried mushrooms, which have an excellent flavor, are the kind most frequently called for in this book. They should be soaked in lukewarm water for 15 to 20 minutes before they are used. Stems should not be used.

Onions: Round onions or dry yellow onions may be used. In recipes calling for leeks, onions may be substituted in slightly smaller quantities.

Pork: Uncooked pork is meant unless otherwise specified.

Potatoes: Size should be such that three potatoes equal one pound.

Snow peas: Small green peas used shell and all. They should be strung before they are used.

Spinach: Oriental spinach is smaller in size and more tender than the ordinary Occidental variety and consequently requires less time for cooking.

Vermicelli: The two types of vermicelli called for in this book are not the Italian type but are made from green beans and seaweed, respectively. The type made from beans is called *fên ssŭ* in Chinese and *harusame* in Japanese. It is used in either hot or cold dishes. The seaweed type is called *yang fên* in Chinese and *ito ganten* in Japanese. It resembles gelatine and is best used in cold dishes. Bean vermicelli should be dipped briefly into boiling water before use, while seaweed vermicelli should be soaked for about 20 minutes in lukewarm water. The shiny type of vermicelli is best. Products made from potatoes are poor in quality and dissolve quickly in

hot water. In any case, Oriental vermicelli should not be cooked too long or it will become mushy.

SPICES AND FLAVORINGS. Among the numerous seasonings employed in Chinese cookery, those mentioned below are the most common. They are listed here with general instructions for their use, but in the individual recipes they should be used strictly according to directions in order that the proper flavor will result.

Bean paste *(mien chiang* in Chinese, *miso* in Japanese): Thick, syrupy paste made from soy beans and used for added flavor in such dishes as Pancake Rolls.

Black pepper: Used chiefly for flavoring noodle dishes and soups. Also mixed with salt for dipping pieces of fried or roasted fowl. Some recipes call for black peppercorns and some for ground black pepper. In others, powder made from rolled peppercorns is preferred to ground pepper.

Garlic: Used chiefly for flavoring fish and meats.

Ginger: Fresh ginger is best, but if it is not available, ground ginger may be used. One-eighth teaspoon of ground ginger is equivalent to one tablespoon fresh chopped ginger. For recipes in this book, one slice of ginger is a thin slice about one inch in diameter. To prevent fresh ginger from drying out, bury it in a flower pot filled with moist sand or loose earth. Ginger juice is obtained by grating fresh ginger and squeezing the juice out through a cloth.

Leek (long onion): Use white part only. Cut according to instructions in individual recipes. In this book "stalk" means only four or five inches of the white part.

Monosodium glutamate *(wei ching* in Chinese, *ajinomoto* in Japanese): "Accent," "Ajinomoto," and "Gourmet Powder" are popular brands.

Onion: Round onion may be substituted in slightly smaller amounts in recipes calling for leeks.

Red pepper: Cayenne or chili pepper. Prepared ground variety may be used, but it is preferable to make red pepper powder by toasting chili peppers in a skillet and rolling them into a powder on a board.

Red pepper oil: To prepare, heat three tablespoons of sesame oil, fry three or four red peppers in it until they turn dark, remove peppers, and use oil only. Or mix heated sesame oil with ground or rolled red pepper.

Sesame oil: Used chiefly to give added flavor to vegetables.

Sesame seed: Either black or white variety may be used unless recipe specifies which. Toasting adds interesting flavor but must be done carefully, since sesame seeds burn easily.

Soy sauce: This is as important in Chinese cookery as salt is in most other countries. It imparts a special flavor to foods. Since non-Oriental soy sauces are more concentrated and salty, they should be used in smaller amounts than those indicated in recipes in this book.

Star aniseed: The dry, star-shaped seeds add excellent flavor to beef, pork, and duck.

Sugar: Granulated sugar is meant unless otherwise specified. Since sugar used in the Orient is not so sweet as Occidental sugar, measurements called for in this book should be slightly decreased if latter is used.

Tabasco: This goes well with Chinese food and may be used in place of red pepper in certain of the recipes.

Tomato catsup: Use as indicated in recipes.

Vinegar: Since Western-style vinegar is stronger than the Oriental variety, amounts called for in this book should be slightly decreased if former is used.

Wine: If Chinese yellow wine is unavailable, dry white sherry, cognac, or Japanese saké may be substituted.

SPECIAL HELPS AND HINTS. *Advance preparation:* Preparation of the ingredients for Chinese dishes involves more work than the actual cooking. Much time and energy will be saved if the prepared ingredients are all assembled in one place—preferably on a large platter or plate—before the cooking process is undertaken. Seasonings should be readily accessible. Such advance steps as washing, soaking, cutting, parboiling, and pre-deep-frying should be accomplished first. Once the pan is on the fire, fried foods will require only a few minutes. If advance preparations are made, reheating, deep-frying, or sautéing will take only 15 minutes before serving.

Cutting methods: It is a basic principle of Chinese

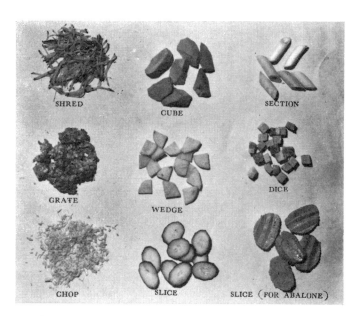

SHRED CUBE SECTION

GRATE WEDGE DICE

CHOP SLICE SLICE (FOR ABALONE)

cooking to cut the ingredients into sizes and shapes convenient for picking up with chopsticks, so that knives and forks need not be used. Meat and vegetables are frequently shredded. A single dish nearly always consists of two or more main ingredients (meat and vegetables or fish and vegetables), and these are always cut to the same size. The following are the chief methods of cutting employed in recipes in this book (see photograph):

Chop: Cut into very small pieces with knife or other implement.

Cube: Cut into cubes approximately one inch in size.

Dice: Cut into small cubes the size of dice.

Flake: Cut or grate into shavings.

Grate: Rub on a grater to produce fine grains.

Mince: Cut fine with knife or kitchen scissors.

Section: Cut into one- to two-inch lengths.

Shred: Cut into fine, thread-like strips.

Slice: Cut into very thin pieces. (Abalone should be sliced in a wavy pattern.)

Wedge: Cut into small triangular sections.

Chinese cooking techniques: Braise: Brown ingredients in small amount of oil, add broth or water, cover tightly, and cook slowly (30 to 90 minutes, depending on ingredients) over weak flame until ingredients become tender. Braised dishes may be prepared in extra portions to be served at subsequent meals. This saves effort for the cook. Extra portions need only to be steamed before they are served.

Deep-fry: Fry ingredients with or without batter in plenty of deep oil.

Dredge: Sprinkle or coat with flour, cornstarch, soy sauce, or other substances before cooking.

Fry (or sauté): Cook in small amount (3 to 6 tablespoons) of hot oil.

Fu yung: Cook with eggs to give omelet effect.

Mix: Combine ingredients, usually by stirring.

Sauté: See Fry.

Smoke: Soak meat in seasonings, then smoke over brown sugar or pine needles. This method may be substituted for deep-frying in some recipes.

Steam: Arrange food on plate or rack and steam over boiling water for 15 minutes to 1 hour.

Sweet and sour dishes: Make sauce by mixing ingredients with small amount of cornstarch and pour sauce over main ingredients.

Cornstarch: Cornstarch is used with great frequency in Chinese cooking to thicken the gravy or sauce and to make it more palatable. The use of cornstarch also serves to keep the food hot for a longer time and enhances its appearance by making it more glossy. In most cases, cornstarch is mixed with water before it is added to the other ingredients. Follow instructions in individual recipes.

Measurements: The measurements in these recipes should be strictly adhered to. If desired, they may be decreased, but never increased. In this book

    1 cup equals 1/2 pint or 200 cubic centimeters

    1 tablespoon equals 1/2 fluid ounce or 15 cubic centimeters

    1 teaspoon equals 1 1/3 fluid drams or 5 cubic centimeters

For other information on measurements, see "Sizes and Amounts of Ingredients."

Oil: Since Chinese cooking requires a large amount

of frying oil, it is sometimes uneconomical to use prepared oils. Also, since vegetable oils are always preferred to animal fats in Chinese cooking, peanut oil and bean oil —popular products of China and Japan—are most often used. Cottonseed oil is a satisfactory substitute. If vegetable oil is used, the food remains delicious even if it becomes cold. On the other hand, if lard is used, the food should be served hot. When you use peanut, bean, or cottonseed oil, it should first be purified as follows:

1. Pour 5 cups of oil into a pan and add 3 slices of ginger and 1 leek cut into 3 sections.

2. Heat oil until ginger and leek turn brown; then remove them. Oil is then ready for use.

Heating the oil in this fashion imparts a special flavor. When you prepare hot or cold dishes, it is wise to add a few tablespoons of sesame oil for a richer flavor. Sesame oil does not require purification before use. Chinese food is rich but not greasy.

Here are further suggestions regarding the use of oil:

1. The cooking pan should be well heated before the oil is put in.

2. The oil should be well heated before ingredients are added.

3. Ginger, leek, and garlic should be browned slightly before other ingredients are added.

4. Deep-fry oil can be used over and over again if it is poured through a strainer lined with a piece of cotton. The cotton can then be discarded, and the strainer will be easy to clean. Before each use, brown 4 slices of ginger and 5 inches of leek in the oil to remove odor. Keep oil in a covered container.

5. If oil spatters when ingredients are added, cover pan with a lid.

Seasoning: When you are preparing meat or fish

dishes, these ingredients should first be partially cooked before you add soy sauce and salt.

If a little salt is first sprinkled into water or oil, boiled or fried vegetables will turn a brighter green.

When a recipe calls for several seasonings, these should first be mixed in a small bowl and placed conveniently by the cooking pan. Seasonings should be added quickly at the proper time indicated in each recipe.

For cold dishes, the sauce should not be added until immediately before serving.

Ginger and garlic should be crushed with the back of a heavy knife.

Servings: Recipes in this book will serve four persons, unless otherwise specified. Instead of increasing portions for additional guests, as one would do in most Western countries, the custom in China is to enlarge the fare with another dish or two.

Stock (or broth): A good soup stock is always essential in the preparation of Chinese food. Stock made from whole soup chicken or pieces of beef or pork is the best. Chicken, beef, and pork bones make a second-class stock. Stock made from beans, fish, dry shrimp, or vegetables may also be used.

Boil the ingredients (chicken, beef, or bones) in plenty of water with 1 stalk of leek and 3 slices of ginger. Cook over low flame and do not cover. Simmer for 1 hour. The stock should be very clear. Add 1/2 teaspoon of mono-sodium glutamate. Remove meat from stock to be eaten separately with soy sauce or used in salad.

Utensils (see photographs, pages 21 and 22): The jack-of-all-trades in Chinese cooking is the coolie-hat pan, which is round at the bottom and is used for both frying and cooking. It is not suitable for use on an electric stove, but other pans may be substituted. If you do not have a Chinese pan, a deep frying pan will do quite well.

A steamer with a rack is another essential. The ones shown in the photograph are made of wood and bamboo. When food is to be reheated, it is much better to place it in a steamer than to heat it directly over a flame. When removing a dish from the steamer, first pour cold water inside so that you will not burn your hands.

You will also need a ladle for some of the recipes. The other required utensils will be found in any well-equipped kitchen.

You had better wait for the meat than the meat wait for you.
Chinese proverb

CHICKEN DUCK AND OTHER POULTRY

Empress Chicken
Velvet Chicken and Sweet Corn
Steamed Chicken in Yünnan Pot
Chicken Fu Yung
Steamed Chicken with Pineapple
Spring Chicken with Red and Green Peppers
Rice-stuffed Chicken
Chicken in Wine
Smoked Chicken
Stewed Chestnut Chicken
Fried Chicken
Fried Chicken with Brown Sauce
Fried Chicken with Green Peppers
Fried Chicken Fillet with Peanuts
Fried Chicken with Walnuts
Fried Chicken, Peking Style
Fried Chicken, Paper-wrapped
Jellied Chicken
Cold Chicken with Brown Sauce
Cold Chicken Liver and Giblets
Sliced Cold Chicken
Crisp Roasted Duck
Minced Pigeon
Fried Pigeon
Roast Stuffed Turkey

INGREDIENTS, COMMON AND
EXOTIC

Since the ingredients called for in
this book are those commonly used
in the Orient, they differ occasionally from those known in the West.
Almost all of them, however, can be
obtained without difficulty, and the
more exotic-sounding items are
available at Chinese and Japanese
food stores and restaurants. (See
pages 15 & 16.)

Empress Chicken

Ingredients:

> 6 wings and 6 legs of spring
> chicken (about 2 1/2 lbs.)
> 1 small bamboo shoot, cut
> into small slices
> 1 stalk leek
> 4 slices ginger
> 6 tbsps. oil
> 2 tbsps. wine
> 8 tbsps. soy sauce
> 2 cups broth or water
> 1 tbsp. sugar
> 3 tbsps. green peas
> Dash monosodium glutamate

Method: 1. Wash chicken in warm water. 2. Cut bamboo shoot into small slices and leek into 1/2-inch pieces. 3. Heat oil in pan and fry leek and ginger for a few minutes. Then add chicken and bamboo and continue to fry. 4. When chicken changes color, add wine and soy sauce. 5. Add sufficient broth or water to cover chicken and cook for 20 minutes. 6. Add sugar and turn fire to low flame. Simmer for 1 hour. 7. Add green peas toward end of simmering period. Then add monosodium glutamate and serve hot.

Note: This dish may be cooked beforehand and reheated before serving. To use leftover portion, simply steam it.

Velvet Chicken and Sweet Corn

Ingredients:

> 1/4 lb. minced chicken fillet
> 1 tbsp. wine
> 1 tsp. salt
> 2 egg whites, lightly beaten
> 2 cups chicken broth, with 1/2
> tsp. salt added

> 1 can cream-style sweet corn
> 1 tbsp. cornstarch, mixed with
> 3 tbsps. water
> 1/2 tsp. monosodium glutamate
> 1 tbsp. chopped ham

Method: 1. Mince chicken fillet and mix well with wine, salt, and beaten egg whites. 2. Bring chicken broth to boil, add sweet corn and chicken mixture, and bring to boil again. 3. Add cornstarch and water mixture, stirring constantly for 3 minutes. 4. Add monosodium glutamate, pour soup into deep serving bowl, garnish with chopped ham, and serve hot.

Steamed Chicken in Yünnan Pot

Ingredients :
> 1 spring chicken, disjointed
> 2 tbsps. wine
> 1 stalk leek, cut into small pieces
> 3 slices ginger
> 2 tsps. salt
> 1/2 cup water

Method : This dish requires the use of a Yünnan pot, as shown in the illustration. The pot, which has a central chimney, is placed over a pan of boiling water and covered with a lid, so that the steam rises through the chimney to cook the contents and to produce a soup that is the utmost in deliciousness and nutritional value.

1. Disjoint cleaned chicken and place pieces in Yünnan pot around central chimney. 2. Add all other ingredients, cover with lid, and place pot on top of pan containing sufficient water for at least one hour of boiling. 3. Allow chicken to steam for one hour or until tender. Remove Yünnan pot and serve chicken with soup produced by steaming.

Chicken Fu Yung

Ingredients :

> 1/4 lb. chicken breast, ground *or* chopped
> 3 tbsps. water
> 1 tsp. wine
> 1/2 tsp. salt
> 1 tbsp. cornstarch
> 6 egg whites
> 10 tbsps. oil
> 2 tbsps. oil (preferably from chicken fat)

> *Sauce :*
> 8 small slices bamboo shoot
> 8 snow peas
> 1 cup chicken broth
> 1 tsp. salt
> 1 tbsp. cornstarch
> 1/4 tsp. monosodium glutamate
> 3 tbsps. water

Method : 1. Add 3 tbsps. water to ground chicken breast a few drops at a time and mix well. If ground chicken is not used, chop breast meat very fine, adding a few drops of water at a time while chopping. 2. Add wine, salt, and cornstarch. Mix thoroughly. 3. Beat egg whites until stiff and gradually fold into chicken mixture. (Save yolks for use in a dish that calls for egg yolks only.) 4. Heat 10 tbsps. oil in pan and add chicken mixture. Remove from fire immediately and stir briskly. Replace on fire and cook until firm but not browned. 5. Heat 2 tbsps. oil from chicken fat (or ordinary oil) and sauté bamboo shoot and snow peas. Add 1 cup chicken broth and bring to boil. 6. Mix 1 tsp. salt, 1 tbsp. cornstarch, 1/4 tsp. monosodium glutamate, and 3 tbsps. water. Stir this mixture into sauce. 7. Place chicken mixture in dish, cover with sauce, and serve hot.

Steamed Chicken with Pineapple

Ingredients :
1 spring chicken
Oil for deep-frying
1 stalk leek, cut into small sections
5 slices ginger
1 tbsp. wine
3 tbsps. soy sauce
1 tsp. salt
1 tbsp. sugar
1 cup canned pineapple chunks
1 tbsp. cornstarch
1/2 cup juice from canned pineapple
1/2 cup juice from steamed chicken

Method : 1. Deep-fry whole chicken to golden brown. (Chicken may be halved before deep-frying.) 2. Place chicken in bowl. Add leek, ginger, wine, soy sauce, salt, and sugar. Steam for 40 minutes or until tender. 3. Remove bones and cut chicken into 2-inch pieces. Place on a serving plate. 4. Heat 1/2 cup juice from pineapple and 1/2 cup juice from steamed chicken, adding pineapple chunks and 1 tbsp. cornstarch. 5. When mixture thickens, cover chicken with it and serve hot.

Spring Chicken with Red and Green Peppers

Ingredients :

A
1 spring chicken, cut into pieces about 2 inches square
1 tbsp. wine
1 tbsp. soy sauce
4 tbsps. cornstarch
5 cups oil for deep-frying

B
5 tbsps. oil
1 clove garlic, crushed

3 slices ginger
3 or 4 red peppers, cut in half
5 green peppers, quartered and seeded
2 tbsps. wine
1 tsp. sugar
4 tbsps. soy sauce
1 tsp. cornstarch, mixed with 1 tbsp. water
Dash monosodium glutamate

Method : 1. Sprinkle chicken first with wine, next with soy sauce, and then with cornstarch from A ingredients. 2. Heat 5 cups oil and deep fry chicken in small amounts until golden brown. Remove chicken to a plate. 3. Heat 5 tbsps. oil; add garlic, ginger, and red peppers. Then add green peppers and fry for 2 minutes. Do not fry green peppers too soft. 4. Add deep-fried chicken, mix well, and continue to fry. Add remaining seasonings from B ingredients. When these boil up, add cornstarch and water mixture. Stir well and serve hot.

Rice-stuffed Chicken

Ingredients:
1 whole chicken (about 2 lbs.)
7 cups water

A	B
1/4 lb. glutinous rice, soaked in water for 10 minutes and drained thoroughly	1 tbsp. sugar
	3 tbsps. wine
	5 tbsps. soy sauce
4 dried mushrooms, soaked and sliced	1 onion, cut into small pieces
2 chicken livers, diced	**C**
1 oz. ham, diced	1 egg
5 arrowhead bulbs or water chestnuts or 1 small bamboo shoot, diced	2 tbsps. soy sauce
	5 tbsps. flour
2 tbsps. soy sauce	
1 tsp. sugar	Oil for deep-frying
1 pinch black pepper	

Method: 1. Heat water to boiling point, lower heat, and add whole chicken. Simmer for 10 minutes until skin contracts. 2. Remove chicken from water and stab it all over with a fork to permit easier absorption of liquid. 3. Mix A ingredients thoroughly, stuff chicken with mixture, and use toothpicks (or metal pins) and string to close opening. 4. Replace chicken in water and add seasonings B. 5. Cover with lid and simmer over weak flame for 1 hour until water has almost completely evaporated. 6. Remove chicken from pan and coat completely with mixture of C ingredients. 7. Heat oil and deep-fry chicken to light golden brown.

Note: Steps 1–5 may be done some time in advance. Steps 6 and 7 may be omitted according to taste. In either case, chicken should be served hot.

Chicken in Wine

Ingredients:

1/2 spring chicken (about 1 lb.)	1 tbsp. salt
1/2 stalk leek	1/2 cup wine
2 slices ginger	1/4 cup soy sauce

Method: 1. Clean chicken, rub with 1 tbsp. salt, place ginger and leek inside, and steam for 30 minutes or until tender. 2. Soak chicken overnight in mixture of wine and soy sauce. 3. Slice chicken and serve cold.

Smoked Chicken

Ingredients :

1 spring chicken

3 tbsps. brown sugar (hung t'ang *in Chinese,* zarame *in Japanese)*

2 tsps. salt

1 tsp. ground or rolled black peppercorns

2 tsps. sesame oil

Method : 1. Boil or steam whole chicken for 40 minutes. 2. Rub chicken inside and out with mixture of pepper and salt. 3. Heat 2 tbsps. brown sugar in an *old* pan. (Sugar will scorch the pan.) 4. Place a wire grill over sugar and set chicken on grill. 5. Cover pan with lid wrapped in paper to keep it clean and to prevent smoke from escaping. 6. Smoke chicken for 10 minutes over low flame. Remove burned sugar, add remaining 1 tbsp. brown sugar, and smoke chicken for another 5 minutes. 7. Remove chicken and rub with sesame oil. 8. Cut into small pieces. Serve hot or cold.

Note : Pine needles may be used instead of brown sugar for smoking chicken. Place a piece of aluminum paper in the pan; then put sugar on the paper. It will keep the pan clean.

Stewed Chestnut Chicken

Ingredients :

1 spring chicken, cut into 1 1/2-
   inch pieces, including bone
2 slices ginger
1 small leek, cut in small sections
1 lb. chestnuts, boiled, shelled,
   and halved
1 tsp. salt
6 tbsps. soy sauce
2 tbsps. wine
2 cups water
1 tbsp. sugar
6 tbsps. oil

Method : 1. Heat oil in frying pan and fry ginger and leek. Then add chicken. 2. When chicken changes color, add salt, soy sauce, wine, and water. 3. Cover with lid and simmer for 40 minutes. Add sugar and chestnuts. 4. Simmer for another 15 minutes and serve hot.

Fried Chicken

Ingredients :

1 spring chicken	3 tbsps. flour
1 leek, cut into small sections	1 egg
5 slices ginger	1/2 tsp. salt
1 tbsp. wine	Several tbsps. chicken broth
2 tbsps. soy sauce	Oil for deep-frying

Method : 1. Cut chicken in half and boil or steam with leek, ginger, wine, and soy sauce until tender. Save broth. 2. Bone chicken and let stand until cold. 3. Make a paste with flour, egg, salt, and small amount of broth from boiled chicken. 4. Coat chicken with this paste and deep-fry in oil until light brown and crisp. Serve immediately.

Fried Chicken with Brown Sauce

Ingredients :

3/4 lb. chicken fillet, cut into small cubes	1 bamboo shoot, cut into small cubes
1 tsp. wine	2 chili peppers, cut into small pieces
1 tsp. cornstarch	Oil for deep-frying
1/2 tsp. salt	3 tbsps. oil
3 dried mushrooms, soaked and diced	3 tbsps. chiang (brown sauce)

Method : 1. Dredge chicken with wine, cornstarch, and salt. 2. Heat deep-fry oil and fry chicken for 2 minutes. Remove to a plate. 3. Heat 3 tbsps. oil and fry mushrooms, bamboo shoot, and peppers. 4. Add 3 tbsps. *chiang.* Then add chicken, stir well, and serve hot.

Fried Chicken with Green Peppers

Ingredients :
  1 lb. chicken fillet, cubed
  2 tsps. wine
  1/2 egg white
  1 tsp. cornstarch
  9 small green peppers, seeded and
    cut into small squares
  8 tbsps. oil
  2 tsps. salt
  1/2 tsp. sugar
  1/2 tsp. monosodium glutamate

Method : 1. Mix cubed chicken fillet with 1 tsp. wine, 1/2 egg white, and 1 tsp. cornstarch. 2. Heat 5 tbsps. oil and fry chicken until color turns. 3. Remove chicken to a plate and clean frying pan. 4. Heat remaining 3 tbsps. oil and fry green peppers for 3 minutes, stirring well during process. 5. Add fried chicken, salt, sugar, 1 tsp. wine, and monosodium glutamate. 6. Remove from flame and serve hot.

Note : For extra flavor, either diced mushrooms or diced bamboo shoot may be added.

Fried Chicken Fillet with Peanuts

Ingredients :

A
  1 lb. chicken fillet, cut into
    small cubes
  1 tsp. cornstarch
  1/2 egg white
  1 1/2 tbsps. water

B
  1 tbsp. wine
  3 tbsps. soy sauce
  1/2 tsp. salt
  1/2 tsp. sugar

  1 tsp. cornstarch, mixed with
    1 tsp. water

C
  1 clove garlic, cracked
  2 slices ginger
  4 chili peppers, halved
  1 stalk leek, cut into small pieces

  8 tbsps. oil

  1 cup raw peanuts, skinned (or
    unsalted roasted peanuts)
  Oil for deep-frying

Method : 1. Cube chicken fillet and mix with other A ingredients. 2. Mix B ingredients in separate dish. 3. Heat oil and deep-fry raw peanuts until crisp. Guard against burning. Remove to a plate. (If roasted peanuts are used, do not deep-fry.) 4. Heat 6 tbsps. oil and fry chicken. When meat turns white, remove to a plate. 5. Clean frying pan, heat 2 tbsps. oil, and fry C ingredients for 2 minutes. 6. Add fried chicken and mixture of B ingredients and continue to fry. 7. Stir in peanuts quickly and serve hot.

Chicken, Duck &
Other Poultry

33

Fried Chicken with Walnuts

Ingredients :

   1 lb. boneless spring chicken
     (or chicken fillet), cubed
   1 egg white, unbeaten
   1 tbsp. cornstarch
   2 slices ginger
   6 tbsps. oil
   2 cups English walnut
     meats, blanched
   Oil for deep-frying
   1 tbsp. wine
   1 tsp. sugar
   3 tbsps. soy sauce
   1 tsp. cornstarch, mixed
     with 1 tbsp. water

Method : 1. Cut chicken into 1/2-inch cubes and mix with unbeaten egg white and 1 tbsp. cornstarch. 2. Blanch walnut meats in boiling water for 15 minutes. Or cover meats with cold water, bring to a boil, boil for 3 minutes, and drain immediately. Skins should be removed in this process to eliminate bitter flavor. 3. Heat oil and deep-fry walnuts to light brown. Since walnuts burn easily, they must be removed from oil as soon as color changes. 4. Heat 6 tbsps. oil, add 2 ginger slices and chicken cubes and fry for a few minutes. 5. When chicken changes color, add wine, sugar, and soy sauce. Fry for a few more minutes; then add cornstarch mixture and fried walnuts. Mix well and serve hot.

Fried Chicken, Peking Style

Ingredients :

   1 spring chicken (about 2 lbs.)
   3 tbsps. wine
   5 tbsps. soy sauce
   5 inches leek, chopped
   1 tbsp. ginger juice
   Oil for deep-frying

Sauce:

   3 tbsps. soy sauce
   1 1/2 tbsps. vinegar
   1 tbsp. sesame oil
   1/2 tbsp. sugar
   1/2 stalk leek, chopped
   1 tsp. minced ginger
   1/2 tsp. minced garlic

Method : 1. Soak chicken in mixture of wine, soy sauce, leek, and ginger for at least one hour. 2. Heat oil and deep-fry chicken. 3. Drain chicken and cut into small pieces about 2 inches long. Arrange these artistically on a plate. 4. Mix sauce ingredients thoroughly and pour sauce over chicken before serving.

Fried Chicken, Paper-wrapped

Ingredients :
  1/2 lb. chicken fillet, cut into
     60 small pieces
  30 slices ginger
  30 snow peas
  30 small pieces onion or leek
  1 tbsp. wine
  2 tbsps. soy sauce
  3 or 4 oz. chicken fat (or
     sesame oil or lard)
  30 6-inch squares Cut-rite
     wax paper
  Oil for deep-frying

Method : 1. Combine chicken fillet, ginger, and onion with soy sauce and
wine.   2. Rub a little sesame oil or lard on center of wax-paper squares,
or place small piece of chicken fat on each square.   3. In each square, wrap
two pieces chicken fillet, one piece onion, one slice ginger, and one snow
pea. Fold paper in envelope style as shown in illustration and tuck in flap
to secure.   4. Heat oil and deep-fry wrapped chicken, flap side down, until
light brown in color. Remove from oil and serve hot.   5. Break paper wrapping with chopsticks before eating chicken.

Jellied Chicken

Ingredients :
  1/2 spring chicken (about   3 tbsps. soy sauce
     1 lb.)   1/2 tsp. salt
  1 tbsp. wine   14 black peppercorns
  1 stalk leek (whole)   1 clove star aniseed
  4 slices ginger   1 tbsp. canned green peas

Method : 1. Using sufficient water (about 5 cups) to cover chicken, add
wine, whole leek, ginger, soy sauce, and salt and boil chicken for 30 minutes.
2. Remove bones from chicken and cut meat into 1-inch pieces. Arrange
pieces in deep bowl and allow to cool.   3. Using soup from boiled chicken,
add peppercorns and aniseed and simmer chicken bones for 20 minutes.
4. Remove bones and spices and pour broth over chicken meat in bowl.
Add green peas, allow to cool, and place in refrigerator overnight.   5. Just
before serving, dip bowl quickly into hot water to loosen jellied chicken,
invert bowl on plate, and turn out jellied chicken. Serve in slices.

Note : If extra 1/2 tsp. of salt is substituted for soy sauce, jellied chicken
will be white; otherwise the color is brown.

**Chicken, Duck &
Other Poultry**

35

Cold Chicken
with Brown Sauce

Ingredients :
1 whole spring chicken (about
  2 lbs.)
1/2 stalk leek, cut into small
  pieces
4 slices ginger

A	B
3 tbsps. wine	5 tbsps. soy sauce
1 tsp. ground black pepper	3 tbsps. sesame oil
1 tbsp. salt	1 tbsp. sugar
	1 cup juice from chicken after steaming

Method : 1. Mix A ingredients and rub chicken inside and out with mixture. Place leek and ginger inside chicken. 2. Place chicken in bowl and steam over high flame for 30 minutes. 3. Heat B ingredients in a pan. Then add steamed chicken and bring mixture to a boil. Turn chicken constantly until color changes. 4. Cool chicken and cut into pieces about the size of 1 1/2-inch cubes. Garnish with parsley and serve cold.

Cold Chicken Liver and Giblets

Ingredients :

1 lb. chicken livers	1 tsp. black peppercorns
1 lb. chicken giblets	1 cup soy sauce
6 slices ginger	1/2 cup wine
1/2 stalk leek	2 tbsps. sugar
2 cloves aniseed	

Method : 1. Wash chicken livers and giblets. Fill a saucepan with sufficient water to cover livers and giblets and bring to a boil. When water is boiling, add livers and giblets. When it boils up again, drain livers and giblets, discarding water. 2. Place all other ingredients in pan, add livers and giblets, and boil for 10 minutes. 3. Remove livers and boil giblets 20 to 40 minutes longer. 4. Slice livers and giblets and serve cold.

Sliced Cold Chicken

Ingredients :

1 spring chicken	5 tbsps. wine
1 leek	1 tbsp. salt
5 slices ginger	

Method : 1. Clean chicken, rub inside and outside with salt and wine, and place leek and ginger inside. 2. Steam for 30 minutes or until tender. 3. When chicken has cooled, remove skin and slice chicken very thin. 4. Serve cold with soy sauce.

Crisp Roasted Duck

Ingredients:

1 tender spring duck (about 3 lbs.)
2 tbsps. wine
1 1/2 tbsps. salt
1/2 tbsp. sugar
2 tsps. red pepper powder (from toasted, rolled red peppers)
1 stalk leek
6 slices ginger
4 cloves aniseed
1 egg
3 tbsps. flour

Oil for deep-frying

Condiments:
1/2 tbsp. black pepper (from rolled peppercorns)
1/2 tbsp. salt
2 tbsps. catsup

Method: 1. Sprinkle duck with wine and allow to stand for a while. 2. Mix salt, sugar, and red pepper powder. Rub duck with mixture. 3. Place duck in a large bowl with leek, ginger, and aniseed and steam for 1 to 1 1/2 hours until tender. Remove duck from steamer and allow to cool. 4. Beat egg lightly, add flour, and mix well. Coat duck with this mixture and deep-fry until it becomes crisp (about 15 minutes). 5. Place condiments in two separate dishes, with salt and black pepper mixed together in one and catsup in the other. 6. Serve duck while it is very hot and crisp. Pieces of duck are dipped in condiments before they are eaten.

Minced Pigeon

Ingredients:

1 cup (about 10 oz.) minced pigeon meat
1 tbsp. wine
2 tbsps. water
1/2 tbsp. cornstarch
1/4 cup dried mushrooms, soaked and chopped
1/4 cup chopped bamboo shoot

1/4 cup chopped celery
3 tbsps. oil
1/2 tsp. salt
1/2 tsp. sugar
1 1/2 tbsps. soy sauce
1/2 tbsp. cornstarch, mixed with 3/4 cup water
12 lettuce leaves

Method: 1. Mix minced pigeon meat with wine, water, and cornstarch. 2. Heat 3 tbsps. oil and sauté mixture. Add vegetable ingredients and seasonings. Thicken with cornstarch mixture. 3. Serve in individual portions on lettuce leaves.

Note: Chicken may be substituted for pigeon meat.

Fried Pigeon

Ingredients:

2 pigeons (about 2 lbs.)
1 tsp. black pepper (from rolled peppercorns)
2 tbsps. soy sauce
1 tsp. salt
2 tbsps. honey
Oil for deep-frying

Method: 1. Rub cleaned pigeons inside and out with black pepper, soy sauce, and salt. Rub outside also with honey. 2. Heat oil and fry pigeons until brown. 3. Cut into small pieces and serve hot.

Roast Stuffed Turkey

Ingredients:

1 small turkey (3–5 lbs. before stuffing)

Stuffing:
1/2 lb. ham, cooked and diced
1/2 lb. calf's liver, cooked and diced
1/2 cup diced bamboo shoot
1/2 cup diced celery
1 cup chestnuts, boiled and diced
2 tsps. ginger juice
2 tbsps. soy sauce
1 tsp. sugar
1/4 tsp. monosodium glutamate

Gravy:
2 tbsps. soy sauce
2 tbsps. sesame oil
1 clove garlic, crushed
1 tbsp. ginger juice
1 tbsp. cornstarch, mixed with 1 cup water
1/2 tsp. monosodium glutamate
Salt to taste

Method: 1. Rub turkey inside and out with salt, wash in warm water, and wipe dry with cloth. 2. Mix all stuffing ingredients, stuff turkey, and fasten with toothpicks (or metal pins) and string. 3. Rub turkey with oil and salt, place in roasting pan, and roast in oven at 300° F, allowing about 25 minutes per pound. Raise oven temperature during last hour of roasting. 4. Mix all gravy ingredients and heat to boiling point.

FISH

Fried Fish Fillets
Fried Fish Rolls
Crisp-fried Fish
Fried Fish Balls
Meat-stuffed Fish
Soft-bone Fish
Sweet and Sour Fish
Sweet and Sour Sliced Fish
Steamed Fish with Sweet-sour Sauce
Smoked Fish
Braised Salmon with Soy Beans
Fish with Bean Curd

Fried Fish Fillets

Ingredients:
- 1/2 lb. fish fillets
- 2 tbsps. wine
- 1/2 tsp. salt
- Dash pepper
- 1 tbsp. cornstarch
- 1 egg white, beaten with
  1 tbsp. cornstarch
- Oil for deep-frying

Method : 1. Cut fish fillets into pieces 1 1/2 inches long and 1/2 inch wide. 2. Sprinkle pieces first with wine, next with salt and pepper, and last with cornstarch. 3. Beat egg white, adding 1 tbsp. cornstarch, until mixture is stiff but not dry. 4. Heat oil, dip pieces of fish into egg white, and deep-fry until done. Do not allow egg-white coating to turn brown. Serve fish with salt and pepper.

Fried Fish Rolls

Ingredients :
- 1/2 lb. any white fish or
  fish fillets
- 1 tbsp. ginger juice
- 1/2 tsp. salt
- 4 slices ham, shredded
- Small amount spinach,
  shredded

Coating batter:
- 1 cup flour
- 1 egg
- 2/3 cup water
- 1 tbsp. sesame seeds
- Oil for deep-frying

Method : 1. If fish fillets are not used, clean and bone fish. Cut into pieces 4 inches long and 1 1/2 inches wide. 2. Dredge fish with ginger juice and salt. 3. Using shredded ham and spinach for filling, form fish into rolls and fasten with toothpicks. 4. Mix coating batter, adding sesame seeds last. 5. Coat fish rolls with batter and fry in deep oil. Serve hot.

Crisp-fried Fish

Ingredients:
6 small fish
1/2 cup soy sauce
1/2 tbsp. wine
1 clove aniseed
6 slices ginger
Oil for deep-frying
1 tbsp. sesame oil

Method: 1. Scale and clean fish. Soak in mixture of soy sauce, wine, aniseed, and ginger for 30 minutes. Wipe fish after removing from mixture. 2. Heat oil and deep-fry fish until crisp. 3. Sprinkle fish with sesame oil and serve cold.

Fried Fish Balls

Ingredients:

A	B
1/2 lb. white-meat fish, boned and ground	Sweet and sour sauce:
1/2 cup water	1 tbsp. soy sauce
1 egg white	1/2 tbsp. vinegar
1 tbsp. cornstarch	1/2 tbsp. sugar
1 tsp. wine	1/2 tbsp. cornstarch, mixed with
1/2 tsp. salt	1/2 cup water
1/2 tsp. ginger juice	
Dash monosodium glutamate	**C**
Oil for deep-frying	1/2 tbsp. black pepper
	1/2 tbsp. salt

Method: 1. Clean and bone fish. Using meat grinder, grind fish, gradually adding 1/2 cup water while grinding. 2. Beat egg white, adding cornstarch. Add ground fish, wine, and seasonings (A) and mix thoroughly. Using a teaspoon, form mixture into balls. 3. Heat oil and deep-fry fish balls to golden brown. Serve hot. 4. Heat sauce ingredients B, mixing cornstarch with water before adding to other ingredients. Serve sauce hot in separate bowl. 5. In small separate dish, mix C ingredients. This mixture may be used in place of sauce for dipping fish balls.

Meat-stuffed Fish

Ingredients:
  1 whole fish (carp), 2–2 1/2
    lbs. before cleaning

A
Stuffing:
  4 oz. ground pork
  2 tbsps. chopped leek
  1 tsp. ginger juice
  2 tbsps. cornstarch
  1 tbsp. wine
  1 tsp. sugar
  1 tbsp. soy sauce
  Dash monosodium glutamate

  6 tbsps. oil

B
  2 cups water (more or less)
  1 tbsp. sugar
  3 tbsps. soy sauce
  5 slices ginger
  1 stalk leek, cut into small pieces
  1 clove garlic, cracked

Method: 1. Clean fish and slash crosswise in three places on each side. 2. Mix A ingredients thoroughly and stuff fish with mixture. 3. Heat 6 tbsps. oil and fry fish on both sides until golden brown. 4. Mix B ingredients in cooking pan, using enough water to cover fish, and bring mixture to a boil. 5. Place fish in mixture of B ingredients and cook over medium flame for 25 minutes. 6. Turn to other side and simmer for 10 minutes. Serve hot.

Soft-bone Fish

Ingredients:
  2 lbs. small fish (3 to 5 inches long)
  6 stalks leek, cut into small pieces
  1 large ginger root, sliced
  2 cups vinegar
  1 1/2 cups soy sauce
  5 tbsps. sugar
  3/4 cup sesame oil
  Dash monosodium glutamate

Method: 1. Clean fish by removing intestines and scaling. 2. Mix all other ingredients and simmer fish in this mixture for 2 hours. 3. Remove fish from liquid and serve cold. Bones should be soft enough to eat.

Note: It is advisable to make a large quantity of this dish at one time and use it for later meals.

Sweet and Sour Fish

Ingredients:

A

1 whole fish (carp or any yellow-
 meat fish), about 1 1/2 lbs.
 before cleaning
2 tbsps. wine
3 tbsps. cornstarch
3 tbsps. flour
Oil for deep-frying

B

Sauce vegetable ingredients:
1/2 small bamboo shoot (1/2
 oz.), shredded
3 small dry mushrooms, soaked
 and shredded
1 inch carrot, shredded

3 tbsps. green peas
3 slices ginger
1 clove garlic
4 tbsps. oil

C

Sauce:
5 tbsps. sugar
3 tbsps. vinegar
2 tbsps. soy sauce
1 tbsp. tomato sauce
1 tsp. salt

D

1 tbsp. cornstarch
1 cup cold water

Method: 1. Clean fish, remove entrails, and scale. Score both sides with 3 lines. 2. Rub fish inside and out with mixture A (wine, cornstarch, flour). 3. Heat deep-fry oil. Fry fish until crisp and golden brown (about 15 minutes). 4. Shred bamboo, mushrooms, and carrot. 5. Heat 4 tbsps. of oil in frying pan; fry all sauce vegetable ingredients (B). 6. Pour in sauce mixture C. When sauce boils, add cornstarch mixture D and stir constantly until sauce turns thick. 7. Keep sauce hot and pour over fish. Serve hot.

Note: Fish may be deep-fried in advance. Refry before serving. Fish then becomes more crisp. Any of sauce vegetables may be omitted.

Sweet and Sour Sliced Fish

Ingredients:
1 lb. fish (carp or any white-meat
 fish)

A

4 tbsps. cornstarch
2 tbsps. wine
1 tsp. ginger juice
2 tbsps. soy sauce

Oil for deep-frying

3 tbsps green peas
1/2 cup diced carrots
3 tbsps. oil

B

Sauce:
5 tbsps. sugar
4 tbsps. soy sauce
4 tbsps. vinegar
1/2 tsp. salt
1 tbsp. sesame oil

C

1 tbsp. cornstarch
1 cup water

Method: 1. Remove entrails from fish and scale. 2. Slice fish into two big parts. Slice big parts into 4 or 5 small parts. Score 2 lines on each part.

3. Dip fish into mixture A (cornstarch, wine, ginger juice, soy sauce). 4. Fry in deep oil until crisp and brown. 5. Heat 3 tbsps. oil; sauté green peas and carrots; add B ingredients. 6. Pour in cornstarch mixture C when sauce boils up. Stir constantly. 7. Pour sauce over fried fish. Serve hot.

Steamed Fish with Sweet-sour Sauce

Ingredients:

2 small sea bream or other white-meat fish
1 tbsp. wine
1 tsp. salt
1 tsp. ginger juice
1 small green pepper, seeded and diced
2 red peppers, cut into small pieces

4 slices ginger
1 tbsp. sliced cucumber pickle
2 tbsps. oil
2 tbsps. vinegar
2 tbsps. sugar
1 tbsp. soy sauce
2 tbsps. sesame oil
2 tsps. cornstarch
1 cup water

Method: 1. Clean and scale fish. Make three crosswise slashes on each side. 2. Place fish on plate and sprinkle with wine, salt, and ginger juice. 3. Place plate in steamer and steam fish for 15 minutes. 4. Heat 2 tbsps. oil and fry green pepper, red pepper, ginger, and cucumber pickle. Then add vinegar, sugar, soy sauce, and sesame oil. 5. Mix cornstarch with water, add to sauce mixture, and bring to boil. 6. Cover fish with sauce and serve hot.

Fish

47

Smoked Fish

Ingredients :
1 lb. fish, sliced

A	B
4 tbsps. wine	*Sauce:*
1/2 cup soy sauce	*2 tbsps. wine*
5 slices ginger	*3 tbsps. soy sauce*
2 tbsps. chopped onion	*2 tbsps. sugar*
1 clove garlic, cracked	*2 tbsps. sesame oil*
Dash pepper	*3 tbsps. brown sugar (hung*
2 cloves aniseed	*t'ang in Chinese, zarame in*
1 tsp. black peppercorns (op-	*Japanese)*
tional)	
Oil for deep-frying	

Method : 1. Soak fish in mixture of A ingredients for at least 3 hours or overnight. 2. Heat oil and deep-fry fish piece by piece until golden brown. 3. Heat mixture of B ingredients until it comes to a boil. 4. Dip fried fish slices into sauce and serve hot or cold. 5. If desired, fish may be smoked with brown sugar (or with pine needles) in same manner as Smoked Chicken (see page 31).

Note : If fish is smoked, use an *old* pan and place sugar or pine needles on piece of aluminum foil. Wrap lid in newspaper. This dish may be prepared in advance and kept for 3 or 4 days.

Braised Salmon with Soy Beans

Ingredients :
- 4 slices fresh salmon (about 1 1/2 lbs.)
- 1 stalk leek, cut into small sections
- 4 slices ginger
- 1 cup soy beans
- 2 tbsps. wine
- 3 tbsps. soy sauce
- 1 tbsp. sugar
- 5 tbsps. oil

Method : 1. Soak soy beans overnight. One cup will increase to 2 1/2 cups. 2. Heat oil and fry fish to light brown on both sides. 3. Add leek, ginger, wine, soy sauce, sugar, and soy beans. Cover with lid and simmer for 15 minutes. Serve either hot or cold.

Note : Salted salmon may be used instead of fresh salmon.

Fish with Bean Curd

Ingredients :

A	B
1 lb. fish, cut into bite-size pieces	2 cakes bean curd, cut into 1-inch squares
5 tbsps. oil	4 tbsps. soy sauce
1 tbsp. wine	1 tbsp. sugar
2 tbsps. soy sauce	2 tbsps. wine
1 stalk leek, diced	1/2 tsp. salt
3 slices ginger	Dash monosodium glutamate
	5 small red peppers or a few drops of tabasco

Method : 1. Clean and scale fish, wash, and wipe. Cut into bite-size pieces. 2. Heat 5 tbsps. oil and fry fish. 3. Add remainder of A ingredients and simmer for 10 minutes. 4. Add bean curd and other B ingredients and simmer for 15 minutes. Serve hot.

CHINESE CABBAGE

MELON

GIANT WHITE RADISH

NO. 2 CAN

CELERY

ROUND CABBAGE

CARROT

BAMBOO SHOOT

CARROT

SPRING ONIONS

CUCUMBER

GREEN PEPPER

LEEK

GARLIC

RADISHES

POTATO

TOMATOES

SNOW PEAS

GINGER ROOT

CHILI PEPPERS

SPINACH

ROUND ONION

BECHE-DE-MER

ARROWHEAD BULBS

LIMA BEANS

SESAME SEED

DRIED SHRIMP

STRING BEANS

DRIED SCALLOPS

BIRDS' NESTS

DRIED MUSHROOMS

BEEF LIVER

CHICKEN LIVER

CHICKEN GIBLETS

PORK

SHARK'S FINS

BEEF

BOILED HAM

CHICKEN FILLET

CHINESE CABBAGE

MELON

GIANT WHITE RADISH

NO. 2 CAN

CELERY

ROUND CABBAGE

CARROT

BAMBOO SHOOT

CARROT

SPRING ONIONS

GREEN PEPPER

CUCUMBER

LEEK

GARLIC

RADISHES

GINGER ROOT

SNOW PEAS

TOMATOES

POTATO

SPINACH

CHILI PEPPERS

ROUND ONION

BECHE-DE-MER

ARROWHEAD BULBS

DRIED SHRIMP

SESAME SEED

LIMA BEANS

STRING BEANS

DRIED SCALLOPS

BIRDS' NESTS

DRIED MUSHROOMS

BEEF LIVER

CHICKEN LIVER

CHICKEN GIBLETS

PORK

SHARK'S FINS

BEEF

BOILED HAM

CHICKEN FILLET

SHRIMP AND OTHER SEA-FOOD

Fried Shrimp Balls
Fried Shrimp with Fried Bread
Fried Shrimp with Green Peas
Chilled Bean Curd with Shrimp
Shrimp in Tomato Catsup Sauce
Barbecued Shrimp
Steamed Shrimp Rolls
Braised Shrimp with Bean Curd
Shrimp Toast
Shrimp Cakes
Shrimp-stuffed Mushrooms
Fried Sliced Prawns
Fried Prawns with Chili Pepper Sauce
Fried Prawns with Egg White Batter
Fried Prawns with Tomato Sauce
Steamed Prawns
Crab Fu Yung
Braised Crab Meat and Vegetables
Sliced Cold Abalone
Braised Abalone with Champignons
Abalone with Asparagus and Chicken
Dried Scallops with Radish Balls
Dried Scallops with Eggs
Chilled Cuttlefish
Bêche-de-mer with Sweet-sour Sauce
Fried Oysters
Braised Shark's Fins

HORS D'OEUVRES (1)

Tasty and attractively arranged hors d'oeuvres lend a striking accent to a cocktail party or serve as a pleasant prologue to a dinner party. The photograph shows nine dishes that will delight guests on either of these occasions.

Center: Boiled Eggs with Soy Sauce (page 103)

Lower center: Smoked Fish (page 48)

Upper center: Sliced Cold Beef (page 77)

Right center: Chilled Sweet and Sour Cucumbers (page 120)

Left center: Sliced Ham

Lower right: Sautéed Shrimp

Extreme upper right: Braised Mushrooms (page 116)

Extreme left: Chicken in Wine (page 30)

Top: Sweet and Sour Chinese Cabbage Rolls (page 126)

Fried Shrimp Balls

Ingredients :

1 lb. shrimp, shelled and minced	1 tsp. salt
3 water chestnuts, chopped (or	1 tsp. cornstarch
1/2 cup chopped bamboo shoot)	1 tsp. wine
1/2 tsp. minced ginger	Oil for deep-frying
1 egg white, unbeaten	

Method : 1. Mix all ingredients well. Shape mixture into balls with a tea-spoon. 2. Heat oil and deep-fry shrimp balls to golden brown. Serve hot.

Note : To remove black vein from shrimp, use a toothpick. Stick through the back and lift up, as shown in photograph below.

Fried Shrimp with Fried Bread

Ingredients :

1 lb. shrimp	Oil for deep-frying
1 tsp. wine	5 tbsps. oil for frying shrimp
1/2 tsp. salt	3 tbsps. tomato catsup
1 tbsp. cornstarch	1/2 tsp. sugar
3 slices bread, cut into pieces of	1 tsp. salt
same size as shrimp	

Method : 1. Remove shells and heads of shrimp. Take out black veins. 2. Sprinkle shrimp first with wine, next with salt, and then with cornstarch. 3. Heat deep-fry oil and fry bread cubes until crisp and brown. Remove bread to a plate. 4. Heat 5 tbsps. oil and fry shrimp. When color changes, add catsup, sugar, and salt. Stir constantly for 2 minutes. 5. Add fried bread cubes, mix well, and serve hot.

Fried Shrimp
with Green Peas

Ingredients:
   1/2 lb. shelled shrimp
   1 tsp. wine
   1/2 egg white, unbeaten
   2 tsps. cornstarch
   1 tsp. sugar
   1 1/2 tsps. salt
   1 tbsp. wine
   4 tbsps. green peas (canned
      or parboiled)
   6 tbsps. oil

Method: 1. Remove black line from shrimp, wash, and wipe. 2. Combine shrimp with wine, egg white, and cornstarch. 3. Heat 6 tbsps. oil and sauté shrimp. When color changes, add sugar, salt, wine, and green peas. Mix well. 4. Serve hot in ordinary dish or place in tangerine shells to add attractiveness. (Sliced bamboo shoot and mushrooms may be added.)

Chilled Bean Curd with Shrimp

Ingredients:
   2 cakes bean curd (about 1 lb.)   *2 tbsps. soy sauce*
   1/2 cup dried shrimp, soaked in   *1/4 tsp. monosodium glutamate*
      lukewarm water for 10 minutes   *1 tbsp. sesame oil*
   2 tbsps. chopped leek

Method: 1. Place bean curd on plate and cover with shrimp. 2. Sprinkle with leek, soy sauce, monosodium glutamate, and sesame oil. 3. Chill before serving.

Shrimp in Tomato Catsup Sauce

Ingredients:
   1 lb. shrimp   *Sauce:*
   1 tsp. wine   *2 tsps. salt*
   2 tsps. cornstarch   *2 tsps. sugar*
   Oil for deep-frying   *4 tbsps. tomato catsup*
   3 tbsps. oil   *1 tbsp. cornstarch, mixed with*
   2 tsps. chopped ginger   *3/4 cup water*
   5 tbsps. chopped onion

Method: 1. Wash and shell shrimp. Remove black vein from each. 2. Dredge shrimp with 1 tsp. wine and 2 tsps. cornstarch. 3. Heat oil and deep-fry shrimp for a few seconds. Remove from oil and drain. 4. Heat 3 tbsps. oil, fry chopped ginger and onion, stir well, and add shrimp. 5. Mix sauce ingredients and add to shrimp, stirring constantly. When mixture thickens, remove from flame and serve hot.

Barbecued Shrimp

Ingredients :
    1 lb. shrimp
    1 tsp. ginger juice
    4 tbsps. chopped leek
    2 tbsps. wine
    2 tbsps. soy sauce
    1/2 tsp. salt
    2 tbsps. sugar
    1/6 tsp. monosodium gluta-
        mate
    1 tbsp. sesame oil

Method : 1. Wash shrimp and remove legs but not shells. 2. Cut slit in back of each shrimp and remove black vein. 3. Soak shrimp in mixture of all remaining ingredients for 15 minutes. 4. Remove from mixture and bake in oven for 10 minutes or fry in 6 tbsps. oil. Serve cold.

Steamed Shrimp Rolls

Ingredients :
    1 lb. shrimp, shelled

A

1 tsp. salt
1 egg white (Use yolk in B mixture.)
1 tsp. wine
1 tsp. cornstarch

B

4 eggs (Leave 1 egg white to use in paste.)
1 egg yolk (from A ingredients)
1/2 tsp. salt

4 oz. spinach, dipped in boiling water until tender
2 slices boiled ham or equal amount boiled carrot, cut in strips
1 tbsp. cornstarch
1 tbsp. cornstarch, mixed with 1 egg white (from B) to form paste

Method : 1. Shell shrimp, removing black veins, and chop fine. 2. Mix shrimp with A ingredients and divide mixture into 4 parts. 3. Beat eggs lightly and add salt (B ingredients). Heat small quantity of oil and fry 4 thin egg sheets in roughly oblong shape. 4. Place each egg sheet on board and spread with shrimp paste. Sprinkle with cornstarch. At opposite ends of egg sheets place strips of ham (or carrot) and spinach. 5. Make egg sheets into rolls by rolling from both ends simultaneously. Seal rolls with mixture of cornstarch and egg white. 6. Wrap rolls separately in cheesecloth and steam for 15 minutes. 7. Remove cheesecloth and cut rolls into slices about 1/2 inch thick. 8. Serve cold with mustard and soy sauce.

Shrimp & Other Sea Food

Braised Shrimp with Bean Curd

Ingredients:

1 lb. shrimp	2 cakes bean curd (about 1 lb.), cut into small squares
1 tsp. ginger juice	1 tbsp. wine
1/2 tsp. salt	2 tsps. salt
1 tsp. cornstarch	1/2 tbsp. sugar
6 tbsps. oil	2 tsps. cornstarch, mixed with 2 tsps. water
5 tbsps. chopped leek	

Method: 1. Wash and shell shrimp. Remove black vein from each. 2. Dredge shrimp with ginger juice, salt, and cornstarch. 3. Heat 3 tbsps. oil, sauté shrimp, and remove to a plate. 4. Heat 3 more tbsps. oil, brown leek, and add bean curd, sautéed shrimp, and seasonings. Boil for 10 minutes, add cornstarch mixture to thicken, and serve hot.

Note: One cup sliced cucumbers may be added to this dish.

Shrimp Toast

Ingredients:

A

1 lb. shrimp, shelled and minced
1 tsp. minced ginger or ginger juice
1 tsp. wine
1 tsp. salt
1 egg white, unbeaten
1 tsp. cornstarch
Dash monosodium glutamate

8 slices bread, cut to sandwich thickness

B

2 tbsps. chopped ham
2 tbsps. chopped parsley

Oil for deep-frying

Method: 1. Mix all A ingredients thoroughly. 2. Trim crusts off bread and cut each slice into 4 equal squares. 3. Shape small mound of A mixture on each square of bread. 4. Sprinkle chopped ham and parsley over mounds of shrimp mixture. Press down lightly to make garnish adhere. 5. Heat oil and deep-fry bread squares, first with shrimp-mixture side down, then with bread side down. Fry until bread turns golden brown. Remove from oil and serve hot.

Note: Shrimp toast makes an excellent hors d'œuvre for a cocktail party.

Shrimp Cakes

Ingredients:

    1 1/2 lbs. shrimp, shelled
        and finely chopped
    1/2 tsp. minced ginger
    1 egg white, unbeaten
    1 1/2 tsps. salt
    1 tbsp. wine
    1 tbsp. cornstarch
    Oil for deep-frying
    1/2 lb. spinach
    5 tbsps. oil
    1/2 tsp. salt
    3 cups stock
    1 tbsp. cornstarch, mixed
        with 3 tbsps. water

Method: 1. Combine shrimp, ginger, egg white, salt, wine, and cornstarch. Shape mixture into small flat cakes about size of tablespoon. 2. Sauté spinach with 5 tbsps. oil, adding 1/2 tsp. salt. Remove to serving plate. 3. Heat oil and deep-fry shrimp cakes to golden brown. Remove from oil, drain, and place in pan. 4. Add stock to shrimp cakes and bring to boil. Simmer for 5 minutes. 5. Remove shrimp cakes from stock and place on top of sautéed spinach. 6. Bring stock to boil again, add cornstarch mixture to thicken, and pour over shrimp cakes. Serve hot.

Shrimp-stuffed Mushrooms

Ingredients:

    1/2 lb. shrimp, shelled
    14 dried mushrooms
    1 unbeaten egg white
    1 tsp. ginger juice
    1 tsp. wine
    1 tsp. cornstarch
    1 tsp. salt

Method: 1. Remove black veins from shrimp and chop fine. 2. Soak mushrooms in lukewarm water for 20 to 30 minutes and remove stems. 3. Mix chopped shrimp with egg white, cornstarch, and seasonings. 4. Stuff mushrooms with mixture and steam for 10 minutes. 5. Serve hot or cold with soy sauce.

Fried Sliced Prawns

Ingredients:

1 1/2 lbs. prawns	1/4 lb. cucumber, sliced
1 tbsp. wine	10 tbsps. oil
1 tsp. salt	Seasonings:
1/2 tsp. cornstarch	1/2 tsp. salt
1/4 lb. bamboo shoot, cut into	1/2 tsp. sugar
small slices	1/2 tsp. monosodium glutamate

Method: 1. Shell prawns and remove black vein from each. Halve prawns and slice each half on bias into 4 small pieces. 2. Sprinkle prawns with wine, then with salt, and finally with cornstarch. 3. Heat 5 tbsps. oil and fry sliced prawns until color changes. Remove to a plate. 4. Heat 5 more tbsps. oil and fry bamboo shoot and cucumbers. 5. Add fried prawns and seasonings. Stir well and serve hot.

Note: Any vegetable like snow peas, carrots, or mushrooms may be substituted for bamboo shoot and cucumbers.

Fried Prawns with Chili Pepper Sauce

Ingredients:

1 lb. prawns	1 clove garlic, cracked
1 tbsp. cornstarch	3 tbsps. oil
Oil for deep-frying	1 tbsp. soy sauce
3 chili peppers, chopped (or a few	1 tbsp. wine
drops tabasco, according to	1 tsp. salt
taste)	2 tbsps. sugar
2 slices ginger	1/4 tsp. monosodium glutamate

Method: 1. Shell prawns, remove black veins, and cut each prawn into 4 pieces. Dredge with cornstarch. 2. Heat oil, deep-fry prawns until color changes, and remove to a plate. 3. Mix soy sauce, wine, salt, sugar, and monosodium glutamate in a bowl. 4. Heat 3 tbsps. oil and fry chili pepper, ginger, and garlic. 5. Add seasoning mixture and bring to a boil. 6. Add fried prawns, stir well, cook for a few minutes, and serve hot.

Fried Prawns with Egg White Batter

Ingredients:

8 prawns	Oil for deep-frying
1/2 tsp. salt	Half-and-half mixture of pepper
2 tbsps. cornstarch	and salt
3 egg whites	Tomato catsup
1/4 tsp. salt	
2 tbsps. cornstarch	

Method: 1. Shell prawns, except for tail. Remove black line from back. 2. Dip prawns into mixture of 1/2 tsp. salt and 2 tbsps. cornstarch. 3. Beat egg whites until stiff, adding 1/4 tsp. salt and 2 tbsps. cornstarch to form batter. 4. Heat oil for deep-frying. Dip prawns in egg-white batter and deep-fry. Egg-white batter should remain white, so do not overfry. 5. Serve with half-and-half pepper and salt mixture and or tomato catsup for dipping.

Fried Prawns with Tomato Sauce

Ingredients :

1 lb. prawns, shelled
6 tbsps. flour
1 egg, lightly beaten
14 tbsps. bread crumbs
Oil for deep-frying
1/2 cup leek, cut into 2/3-inch pieces
1/4 cup bamboo shoot, cut into 2/3-inch cubes
1/4 cup carrots, cut into 2/3-inch cubes
1/4 tsp. minced ginger

1/4 tsp. minced garlic
3 tbsps. oil

Sauce:

2 tbsps. tomato catsup
2 tbsps. sugar
1 tbsp. wine
1 tsp. soy sauce
1 tsp. vinegar
1 tbsp. cornstarch, mixed with 1 cup water

Method : 1. Slit backs of prawns, remove black veins, and pound prawns with back of knife blade. 2. Dip prawns in flour, then in egg and bread crumbs. 3. Heat oil and deep-fry prawns to yellow-brown. Drain and cut into bite-size pieces. Place on serving dish. 4. Heat 3 tbsps. oil and fry leek, bamboo, and carrot, adding ginger and garlic. 5. Mix all sauce ingredients except cornstarch mixture and add to vegetables. 6. Bring to boil and add cornstarch mixture, stirring constantly until mixture thickens. 7. Pour sauce over prawns and serve hot.

Steamed Prawns

Ingredients :

4 prawns
1 tbsp. wine
Salt to taste

Method : 1. Shell and wash prawns, remove black veins, and place prawns on plate. 2. Sprinkle with 1 tbsp. wine. 3. Place prawns in steamer and steam for 20 minutes or until tender. 4. Slice steamed prawns lengthwise into halves and salt to taste.

Note : Steamed prawns form an attractive center for a plate of assorted cold foods.

Crab Fu Yung

Ingredients :

1 cup crab meat, fresh or canned	2 tbsps. cornstarch
1 tsp. ginger juice	7 tbsps. oil
1 tbsp. wine	1 cup milk
4 egg whites	1 tbsp. chopped parsley
3/4 tsp. salt	

Method : 1. Remove fragments of shell from crab meat. 2. Mix crab meat with ginger juice and wine. 3. Beat egg whites until stiff. Add salt and cornstarch. 4. Heat oil and let it spread over frying pan. 5. Mix crab meat and milk with egg white. 6. Pour mixture into frying pan. Stir constantly until it thickens. 7. Remove to plate and sprinkle with chopped parsley. Serve hot.

Braised Crab Meat and Vegetables

Ingredients :

2 crabs	1 tsp. ginger juice
1 lb. green vegetables	1 tbsp. wine
1 1/2 cups broth (or water)	1/2 tsp. cornstarch, mixed with
1 1/2 tsps. salt	1/2 tsp. water
3 tbsps. oil	

Method : 1. Steam crabs for 30 minutes or until tender. Remove meat. 2. Cut vegetables into 3-inch lengths and wash well. 3. Bring broth (or water) to boil, add salt, and boil vegetables until tender. 4. Heat 3 tbsps. oil and sauté crab meat. Add ginger juice and wine. Thicken with cornstarch mixture and add to vegetables. Serve hot.

Sliced Cold Abalone

Ingredients :

1/2 lb. fresh abalone	Sauce:
1 stalk leek	2 tbsps. vinegar
5 slices ginger	3 tbsps. soy sauce
3 tbsps. wine	1 tsp. sugar
1 tbsp. salt	1 tsp. sesame oil
	1/4 tsp. monosodium glutamate

Method : 1. Scrub fresh abalone with brush and salt. Then remove meat from shell. 2. Using plenty of water, boil abalone along with leek, ginger, wine, and salt for 2 hours until meat is tender. 3. Remove meat from water and cut off black spongy part. When cool, slice very thin. 4. Mix sauce ingredients and cover sliced abalone with sauce before serving.

Note : If dried abalone is used, soak it in water for 3 or 4 days before boiling. If canned abalone is used, simply slice and cover with sauce.

Braised Abalone with Champignons

Ingredients:
1 can abalone, sliced
2 small bamboo shoots, sliced
1 can champignons
1 1/2 lbs. lima beans
5 tbsps. oil
1 tsp. salt
1 cup broth
2 tbsps. wine
1 tbsp. cornstarch, mixed with
    1 tbsp. water

Method: 1. Slice abalone and bamboo shoot. Cut champignons in half lengthwise. 2. Shell and parboil lima beans. Remove thin skins. 3. Heat oil, add salt, and sauté abalone, bamboo shoot, champignons, and lima beans. 4. Add broth and wine. Boil for a few minutes and add cornstarch mixture to thicken. Serve hot.

Abalone with Asparagus and Chicken

Ingredients:

2 abalone, fresh or canned	Sauce:
1 No. 2 can asparagus spears	1 tbsp. wine
1/2 lb. chicken fillet	1/2 tsp. salt
1/2 tsp. salt	1/2 tsp. sugar
1/2 tsp. cornstarch	2 cups chicken broth (or water)
2 oz. bamboo shoot, cut into small slices	1 tbsp. cornstarch, mixed with 3 tbsps. water
4 tbsps. oil	1/2 tsp. monosodium glutamate

Method: 1. Clean fresh abalone with brush and salt. Steam for 40 minutes and slice in a wavy pattern. (See photo under "Cutting Methods," page 19.) 2. Halve asparagus spears. 3. Slice chicken fillet into 1-inch squares and sprinkle with 1/2 tsp. cornstarch and 1/2 tsp. salt. 4. Heat 4 tbsps. oil in frying pan and fry chicken slices for 2 minutes. Add abalone and bamboo shoot and continue to fry. 5. Add asparagus and all sauce ingredients except cornstarch mixture and monosodium glutamate. When mixture comes to a boil, add these and serve dish hot.

Note: Canned champignons may be substituted for abalone.

Shrimp & Other
Sea Food

Dried Scallops with Radish Balls

Ingredients :
1 lb. giant white radish, peel-
    ed and cut into balls (or
    30 small round radishes,
    peeled)
10 dried scallops (about 6
    oz.)
5 tbsps. oil
2 tbsps. wine

1 tsp. salt
2 cups chicken broth (or water)

1 tsp. cornstarch, mixed with
    1 tbsp. water
1/4 tsp. monosodium glutamate

Method : 1. Place dried scallops in hot water and soak for 1 hour. Save water. 2. Heat 5 tbsps. oil and fry scallops and radish balls. 3. Add water from soaked scallops, 2 cups broth, wine, and salt. 4. Cover with lid and simmer for 15 minutes or until tender. 5. Add cornstarch mixture and monosodium glutamate, stir well, and serve hot.

Note : Turnip balls may be used in place of radish balls.

Dried Scallops with Eggs

Ingredients :
10 dried scallops (about 2 oz.)   5 eggs
1 cup water   1 tsp. salt
2 tbsps. wine   1/2 tsp. sugar
                                     6 tbsps. oil

Method : 1. Heat 1 cup water to boiling point, add 1 tbsp. wine, and soak dried scallops in mixture overnight. Save water from soaking and strain out any sand or sediment that remains. 2. Beat eggs, adding 1 tbsp. wine, 1 tsp. salt, 1/2 tsp. sugar, and water in which scallops have soaked. Add scallops and mix thoroughly. 3. Heat 6 tbsps. oil and fry mixture, stirring well until eggs are done.

Note : The water in which the scallops have soaked adds excellent flavor to this dish.

Chilled Cuttlefish

Ingredients :

2 cuttlefish	4 tbsps. soy sauce
1 tsp. minced ginger	3 tbsps. vinegar
1/2 tsp. minced garlic	2 tbsps. sugar

Method : 1. Open cuttlefish and remove thin skin on both sides. 2. Slice cuttlefish into 2-inch strips. Score each strip on one side in crisscross pattern. 3. Drop cuttlefish in boiling water and cook for 5 minutes. Drain. 4. Mix remaining ingredients to form sauce. 5. Arrange cuttlefish on plate, pour sauce over them, chill, and serve cold.

Bêche-de-mer with Sweet-sour Sauce

Ingredients :

8 sea cucumbers (sea slugs)	4 tbsps. soy sauce
5 oz. bamboo shoot, cut into small	4 tbsps. sugar
slices	3 tbsps. vinegar
5 leeks, cut into 3-inch lengths	3 tbsps. wine
8 tbsps. oil	1 tbsp. cornstarch, mixed with
1 cup broth (chicken or beef)	1/2 cup water
	Dash monosodium glutamate

Method : 1. Soak sea cucumbers in water for 5 to 7 days and bring to a boil once a day. Change soaking water every day. 2. On third day, split sea cucumbers in half and remove intestines. 3. After soaking is completed, brush away sand, clean thoroughly, and drain. 4. Heat 8 tbsps. oil and fry leek and bamboo slices for 3 minutes. 5. Add sea cucumbers, broth, soy sauce, sugar, vinegar, and wine. 6. Cover with lid and cook for 15 minutes. 7. Add cornstarch mixture and monosodium glutamate, stir well, and serve hot.

Shrimp & Other
Sea Food

65

Fried Oysters

Ingredients:
  1 lb. oysters
  1 tbsp. wine
  1 tsp. salt
  1 cup flour
  1 tsp. baking powder
  4 tbsps. cornstarch
  1 cup water (or less)
  1 tbsp. lard
  Oil for deep-frying

Method: 1. Wash oysters in salt water, boil in clear water for 1 minute, drain, and cool. 2. Dredge oysters with 1 tbsp. wine and 1 tsp. salt. 3. Mix flour, baking powder, cornstarch, water, and lard to form coating batter. 4. Dip oysters into batter and fry in deep oil until light brown. Serve hot.

Braised Shark's Fins

Ingredients:

1/4 lb. refined shark's fins	6 dried mushrooms, soaked and
1 cup crab meat (remove bone and	shredded
separate meat)	2 tbsps. wine
1 leek	3 tbsps. soy sauce
5 slices ginger	1 tsp. sugar
5 cups chicken broth	1/2 tsp. monosodium glutamate
1/4 lb. bamboo shoot, shredded	1 tbsp. cornstarch, mixed with
	1/2 cup water

Method: 1. Soak shark's fins overnight. Boil fins with leek and ginger in plenty of water for 1 hour. Drain and rinse. 2. Boil fins again in chicken broth for 30 minutes. Then add crab meat, bamboo, mushrooms, and seasonings. Simmer for 10 minutes. 3. Thicken with cornstarch mixture and serve hot.

Note: Since shark's fins are a delicate and delicious dish, they are served as a special honor to the guest. Shark's fin soup is a famous main dish for big parties. Prepared (refined) shark's fins are recommended for use, since ordinary ones require daily boiling for a whole week.

BEEF

Fried Beef with Snow Peas
Fried Beef with Cauliflower
Fried Shredded Beef with Onions
Fried Beef with Celery
Shredded Beef with Chili Peppers
Fried Shredded Beef and Potatoes
Beef with Fried Potato Slices
Fried Beef with Green Peppers
Stuffed Chinese Cabbage
Sautéed Sliced Beef
Ground Beef with Fried Vermicelli
Bean Curd with Ground Beef and Chili Peppers
Braised Beef with Turnips
Sliced Cold Beef
Pearl Balls
Barbecued Filet Mignon
Fried Beef Liver
Fried Beef Liver with Vegetables

TABLE SETTING AND ASSORTED
COLD FOODS

This is the proper way to arrange
colorful Chinese dishes and utensils.
The table may be round, oval,
square, or rectangular. The large
dish in the center contains an as-
sortment of cold foods of sufficient
diversity to appeal to a wide range
of taste among the guests at a
luncheon or dinner party.

    Center: Steamed Prawns (page
       61) and Steamed Quail Eggs
       (page 103)
    Black: Braised Mushrooms (page
       116)
    White: Sliced Cold Abalone
       (page 62)
    Brown: Sliced Cold Beef (page
       77)
    Yellow: Sliced Cold Chicken
       (page 36)
    Green: Sliced Cucumbers
    Light brown: Sliced White Pork
       (page 87)

Fried Beef
with Snow Peas

Ingredients :
> 1/2 lb. beef, sliced and cut
>   into bite-size pieces
> 1 tbsp. wine
> 3 tbsps. soy sauce
> 2 tsps. cornstarch
> 6 tbsps. oil
> 1/4 lb. snow peas, strung and
>   boiled
> 1 clove garlic, crushed
> 1/2 tsp. sugar

Method : 1. Dredge beef with 1 tbsp. wine, 1 tbsp. soy sauce, and 2 tsps. cornstarch. 2. Heat 4 tbsps. oil and fry beef. When color changes, remove to a plate. 3. Heat 2 tbsps. oil and fry snow peas. Add beef, garlic, 2 tbsps. soy sauce, and sugar. Mix well and serve hot.

Fried Beef with Cauliflower

Ingredients :

> 1 lb. beef fillet, sliced
> 1 egg white, unbeaten
> 1 tsp. ginger juice
> 2 tbsps. soy sauce
> 2 tsps. cornstarch
> Oil for deep-frying

> 1 small cauliflower, separated
>   and cooked
> 2 oz. snow peas
> 1 tbsp. wine
> Dash black pepper
> 1 tsp. salt
> 5 tbsps. oil

Method : 1. Combine sliced beef with egg white, ginger juice, soy sauce, and cornstarch. 2. Heat deep oil and fry beef until tender; then drain. 3. Heat 5 tbsps. oil and fry snow peas and cauliflower. Add wine, pepper, and salt. 4. Add fried beef and stir well over high flame. Serve hot.

Fried Shredded Beef with Onions

Ingredients :

> 1/2 lb. beef, shredded
> 1 tsp. cornstarch
> 2 tbsps. soy sauce
> 2 dry onions, shredded

> 1 tsp. salt
> 1 tsp. sesame oil
> Dash black pepper
> 6 tbsps. oil

Method : 1. Shred beef and dredge with 1 tsp. cornstarch and 1 tbsp. soy sauce. 2. Shred onions, or cut into half rings. 3. Heat 2 tbsps. oil and fry onions, adding salt. Remove to a plate. 4. Heat remaining 4 tbsps. oil. Pour sesame oil over shredded beef and fry. When meat changes color, add onions, 1 tbsp. soy sauce, and dash pepper, stirring briskly. Serve hot.

Fried Beef
with Celery

Ingredients :
  1/2 lb. beef, shredded
  2 tsps. soy sauce
  1 tsp. cornstarch
  1 lb. celery, shredded
  6 tbsps. oil
  3 tbsps. soy sauce
  1/4 tsp. monosodium glutamate

Method : 1. Shred beef and dredge with 2 tsps. soy sauce and 1 tsp. corn-starch. 2. Remove leaves and tough parts of celery, shred, and boil for a few minutes. Remove from fire and drain. 3. Heat 6 tbsps. oil and fry beef. When color changes, add celery, soy sauce, and monosodium gluta-mate. Serve hot.

Shredded Beef
with Chili Peppers

Ingredients :
  1 lb. loin beef, shredded
  Seasonings:
  3 tbsps. soy sauce
  3 tbsps. wine
  1 tsp. minced garlic
  1 tsp. ginger juice

  1 cup shredded carrot or
    cucumber
  3 chili peppers, seeded and
    shredded
  3 cups oil

Method : 1. Shred beef and mix it with seasonings, allowing these to be absorbed. 2. Shred carrots (or cucumbers) and chili peppers. 3. Heat 3 cups oil, add shredded chili peppers, and fry beef and carrots. 4. Drain off oil and save. Continue frying beef and carrots for 3 minutes longer. Serve hot.

Note : The leftover oil may be used later in preparing another dish.

Fried Shredded Beef and Potatoes

Ingredients :
  1/2 lb. beef, shredded
  1 tbsp. soy sauce
  1 tsp. cornstarch
  1/2 lb. potatoes, shredded
  1/2 stalk leek, shredded
  6 tbsps. oil
  Seasonings:
  2 tbsps. soy sauce
  1/2 tsp. salt
  1/4 tsp. monosodium glutamate

Method : 1. Boil shredded potatoes until barely tender; then drain. 2. Dredge shredded beef with 1 tbsp. soy sauce and 1 tsp. cornstarch. 3. Heat 6 tbsps. oil and fry beef and leek. When beef changes color, add potatoes and stir well. 4. Add seasonings, stir well, and serve hot.

Beef with Fried Potato Slices

Ingredients :
  1/2 lb. beef, cut into 1 1/2-inch cubes
  2 tbsps. soy sauce
  1 tsp. cornstarch
  5 tbsps. oil
  4 potatoes (about 1 lb.)
  5 cups oil for deep-frying
  1 tbsp. wine
  1/4 tsp. monosodium glutamate

Method : 1. Dredge cubed beef with 1 tbsp. soy sauce and 1 tsp. corn-starch. 2. Peel and slice potatoes. Rinse slices in cold water and wipe them. 3. Heat 5 cups oil and deep-fry potatoes to golden brown. Remove to a plate. 4. Heat 5 tbsps. oil and sauté beef. 5. When beef changes color, add fried potatoes, 1 tbsp. wine, 1 tbsp. soy sauce, and 1/2 tsp. monosodium glutamate. Serve hot.

Beef

Fried Beef with Green Peppers

Ingredients:

1/2 lb. beef, shredded	1 tsp. salt
1 tbsp. soy sauce	7 tbsps. oil
1 tsp. cornstarch	1 tbsp. soy sauce
Dash black pepper	Dash monosodium glutamate
6 green peppers, seeded and cut into thin strips	

Method: 1. Dredge shredded beef with mixture of 1 tbsp. soy sauce, 1 tsp. cornstarch, and dash black pepper. 2. Heat 3 tbsps. oil in frying pan and fry green peppers, adding 1 tsp. salt. Remove peppers to a plate. 3. Heat 4 tbsps. oil and fry beef. When meat changes color, add green peppers, 1 tbsp. soy sauce, and dash monosodium glutamate. Fry for about 2 minutes, stirring well. Serve hot.

Stuffed Chinese Cabbage

Ingredients:

A	B
10 inside leaves Chinese cabbage	Sauce:
1/4 lb. ground beef or pork	1 tbsp. soy sauce
1/2 cup chopped onion or leek	1 tbsp. vinegar
1/2 tsp. salt	2 tbsps. sugar
1 tsp. soy sauce	1/4 tsp. monosodium glutamate
1 tsp. cornstarch	2 tsps. cornstarch, mixed with 3 tbsps. water
	1 cup juice from stuffed cabbage after steaming

Method: 1. Boil whole cabbage leaves in water for short time, soak in cold water, and drain thoroughly. 2. Cut leaves into oblong shapes 4 or 5 inches long and 2 inches wide. Save trimmed-off parts. Make 4 slits lengthwise in each leaf. 3. Mix remaining A ingredients well and divide into 10 portions. 4. Place one portion on each leaf, fold leaf over, squeeze bottom edges together and press down lightly so that filling shows through slits. Folded leaf should resemble a mitten. 5. Line a deep plate or bowl with trimmed-off parts of cabbage and pile stuffed cabbage in center. Steam for 15 minutes. 6. Heat sauce mixture B, adding cornstarch mixture last. Stir constantly while heating. Bring to a boil, pour over stuffed cabbage, and serve hot.

Sautéed Sliced Beef

Ingredients:
- 1/2 lb. sliced beef
- 3 tbsps. soy sauce
- 1 tbsp. sesame oil
- 1 tbsp. sugar
- 1 stalk leek, chopped
- 1 tsp. chopped red pepper
- 1/8 tsp. grated garlic

Method: 1. Cut beef into bite-size pieces. 2. Soak beef for 15 minutes in mixture of all remaining ingredients. 3. Remove beef from soaking mixture and sauté in ungreased frying pan over strong flame. When color changes, remove from pan and serve hot.

Note: This dish goes well with Vinegar Sautéed Cabbage.

Ground Beef with Fried Vermicelli

Ingredients:
- 1/2 lb. ground beef
- 1 tbsp. wine
- 3 tbsps. soy sauce
- 2 tsps. cornstarch
- 5 red peppers, chopped
- 1 tbsp. chopped onion
- 1/2 tsp. salt
- 1 oz. vermicelli (fên ssŭ in Chinese, harusame in Japanese)
- Oil for deep-frying
- 4 tbsps. oil
- 1 cup water
- 1/4 tsp. monosodium glutamate

Method: 1. Mix ground beef thoroughly with wine, soy sauce, cornstarch, red peppers, onion, and salt. 2. Quarter vermicelli lengthwise. Heat deep oil and fry vermicelli for 2 minutes. Turn it over and fry for 1 minute. Remove from oil and place in deep dish. 3. Heat 4 tbsps. oil and fry meat mixture. Add 1 cup water and 1/4 tsp. monosodium glutamate, mix well, and pour over fried vermicelli just before serving. Serve hot.

Note: Vermicelli will swell during frying process.

Beef

75

Bean Curd with Ground Beef and Chili Peppers

Ingredients :

2 cakes bean curd (3/4 lb.)
1/4 lb. ground or minced beef
3 tbsps. oil
1 clove garlic, cracked
5 chili peppers, chopped
1 tbsp. chopped leek

2 tbsps. soy sauce
1 tsp. sugar
2 tsps. cornstarch, mixed with
    1/2 cup water or broth
1 tbsp. sesame oil

Method : 1. Cut bean curd into small triangles or mixed geometric shapes. 2. Heat oil and fry garlic, red peppers, and leek. Add meat. 3. When meat changes color, add bean curd, soy sauce, and sugar. 4. Cover with lid and cook for 10 minutes. Then add cornstarch mixture. 5. Turn out into serving dish, sprinkle with sesame oil, and serve hot.

Braised Beef with Turnips

Ingredients :

1 lb. shank or round of beef
3 tbsps. oil
4 cloves garlic, flaked
2 stalks leek, cut into 2-inch
    pieces
1 piece ginger (about 2 oz.),
    flaked
1 tbsp. wine
2 cups water
1 lb. turnips, peeled and cut into
    1-inch cubes or diamond
    shapes
Dash pepper
1/2 tsp. salt
1/2 cup soy sauce
Dash monosodium glutamate

Method : 1. Wash beef and cut into 1 1/2-inch cubes. 2. Heat 3 tbsps. oil and fry beef and garlic until beef changes color. 3. Remove beef to a deep pan. Add leek, ginger, wine, and water. Cover tightly and turn fire low after mixture comes to a boil. Simmer for 1 hour or until beef becomes tender. 4. Add turnips, pepper, salt, and soy sauce. Simmer for another 40 minutes. Add dash monosodium glutamate and serve hot.

Note : If a pressure cooker is used, the time element will be reduced. Leftover portions require only steaming before they are served.

Sliced Cold Beef

Ingredients:

2 lbs. beef, cut into two large
    pieces
2 cups soy sauce

2 tbsps. sugar
1 stalk leek, cut into small pieces
10 slices ginger

Method: 1. Cut beef into two large pieces. 2. Soak beef in mixture of remaining ingredients for at least 1 hour. 3. Add sufficient water to cover beef well, bring to a boil, and simmer for 2 hours. 4. Remove beef to a plate and allow to cool. Slice and serve cold.

Pearl Balls

Ingredients:

1 lb. ground beef
1/4 lb. boiled potato, mashed
2 eggs
1/2 round onion, chopped
1 tsp. sugar
2 tsps. soy sauce
2 tsps. ginger juice
2 tsps. salt
1/2 tsp. monosodium glutamate
2 cups glutinous rice, soaked at
    least 3 hours or overnight

Method: 1. Mix ground beef, mashed potato, eggs, and onion thoroughly. 2. Add all other ingredients except rice and mix thoroughly again. 3. Using a tablespoon, shape mixture into small balls. 4. Drain soaked rice thoroughly and roll meat balls in it until they are well covered. 5. Place meat balls in steamer on a wet cloth and steam for 30 minutes. Serve hot. (They may be served in the steamer if you like.) 6. Mustard and soy sauce in separate dishes may be served with this dish for dipping the meat balls.

Barbecued Filet Mignon

Ingredients:

1 lb. fillet of beef, sliced into
    12 pieces, 1/3 inch thick
Seasonings:
4 tbsps. soy sauce
2 tbsps. wine
1 tbsp. ginger juice

1 tsp. sugar
Dash black pepper
1 bunch spinach, cut into sections
9 tbsps. oil
1 tsp. salt

Method: 1. Soak beef slices in seasonings for at least 1 hour. 2. Heat 6 tbsps. oil and fry beef. 3. Heat remaining oil and fry spinach until it becomes tender. Cut into bite size. Add salt. 4. Place fried spinach on plate and spread fried beef over it. Pour the juice from the fried beef over spinach and beef. Serve hot.

Fried Beef Liver

Ingredients :

1 lb. sliced beef liver, cut into   1 tbsp. soy sauce
   bite-size pieces   1 tsp. salt
1 tsp. ginger juice   4 tbsps. flour
1 tbsp. wine   Oil for deep-frying

Method : 1. Soak liver in mixture of seasonings. 2. Coat with flour and deep-fry to light brown. Serve hot.

Fried Beef Liver with Vegetables

Ingredients :

3/4 lb. sliced beef liver   3 tbsps. oil
1 tsp. ginger   1 round onion, cut into eighths
2 tsps. wine   1/2 cup sliced celery
1/2 tsp. salt   2 tbsps. soy sauce
4 tbsps. flour   1/2 tsp. sugar
Oil for deep-frying

Method : 1. Cut liver into bite-size pieces and soak for 15 to 20 minutes in mixture of ginger, wine, and salt. 2. Coat liver with flour and deep-fry to light brown. 3. Heat 3 tbsps. oil and sauté onion and celery, adding soy sauce and sugar. 4. Add fried liver, stir well, and serve hot.

PORK

Fried Pork with Spring Onions
Fried Bamboo Shoots with Pork
Fried Pork Loin
Fried Cabbage with Pork
Meat-stuffed Mushrooms
Pork Chop Suey with Fried Egg
Bean Curd with Sliced Pork and Chili Pepper Sauce
Barbecued Pork
Sweet and Sour Pork
Gold Coin Pork
Sliced White Pork
Sweet and Sour Meat Balls
Steamed Gold and Silver Pork
Braised Pork with Eggs
Braised Pork with Quail Eggs
Braised Pork with Turnips
Molded Steamed Bean Curd
Steamed Meat Balls
Stewed Meat Balls with Cabbage
Fried Pork Kidneys with Chili Pepper
Chilled Pork Kidneys

SWEET AND SOUR PORK

This colorful combination of pork, vegetables, and pineapple is one of the most delectable and widely known dishes in the repertoire of Chinese cuisine. Although it requires no elaborate technique for its preparation, its appearance upon the dinner table is always a welcome event for those who relish its enticing blend of flavors. The recipe appears on page 86.

Fried Pork with Spring Onions

Ingredients:
- 1/2 lb. pork, shredded
- 2 tbsps. soy sauce
- 1 tbsp. wine
- 1 lb. spring onions
- 5 tbsps. oil
- 1/2 tsp. salt

Method: 1. Mix pork with 2 tbsps. soy sauce and 1 tbsp. wine. 2. Wash onions and cut into 2-inch lengths. 3. Heat 5 tbsps. oil and sauté pork. 4. When pork changes color, add onions and salt. Mix well and remove from heat before onions begin to give off juice. Serve hot.

Fried Bamboo Shoots with Pork

Ingredients:
- 1/2 lb. pork, shredded
- 4 tbsps. soy sauce
- 1 tsp. wine
- 1 tsp. cornstarch
- 1/2 stalk leek, shredded
- 1/2 lb. bamboo shoot, shredded
- 8 tbsps. oil
- 1 tsp. sugar

Method: 1. Dredge shredded pork with 2 tbsps. soy sauce, wine, and cornstarch. 2. Heat 8 tbsps. oil and fry pork with leek. When meat changes color, add bamboo shoot. 3. Add remaining 2 tbsps. soy sauce and 1 tsp. sugar, mix well, and cook for 8 minutes. Serve hot.

Fried Pork Loin

Ingredients:

A
- 6 4-oz. pieces pork loin
- 2 tbsps. soy sauce
- 1 tbsp. wine
- Dash minced garlic
- Dash ginger root juice

2 tbsps. oil for frying

B
- 1 leek, cut into small pieces
- 5 tbsps. soy sauce
- 1 tbsp. sugar
- Dash pepper

Method: 1. Mix all A ingredients and allow meat to soak in mixture for 30 minutes. 2. Heat oil and fry meat till golden brown on both sides. 3. Add B ingredients. Cover and let simmer for 20 minutes over low flame. 4. Cut each piece of pork loin into 4 pieces before serving.

Note: Overcooking the pork will increase the flavor.

Pork

83

Fried Cabbage with Pork

Ingredients :

1/2 lb. pork, shredded
1 lb. round cabbage, shredded
5 tbsps. soy sauce

1 tbsp. wine
1/2 stalk leek, shredded
5 tbsps. oil

Method : 1. Mix shredded pork with 2 tbsps. soy sauce and 1 tbsp. wine.
2. Heat oil and fry pork and leek. When pork changes color, add cabbage
and remaining 3 tbsps. soy sauce. Fry until cabbage becomes tender and
serve hot.

Note : Chinese cabbage may be substituted for round cabbage.

Meat-stuffed Mushrooms

Ingredients :

14 medium-sized mushrooms
1/2 lb. ground pork
1 tsp. salt
1 tsp. soy sauce

1 tbsp. wine
1 tsp. cornstarch
1 tbsp. oil

Method : 1. Soak mushrooms in lukewarm water for 10 minutes and remove stems.   2. Mix all other ingredients thoroughly and stuff mushroom
caps, forming small mounds on top of them.   3. Steam stuffed mushrooms
for 15 minutes.   4. Serve mushrooms with mustard and soy sauce.

Note : Shrimp-stuffed mushrooms are made in the same way by using
chopped shrimp instead of ground pork.

Pork Chop Suey with Fried Egg

Ingredients :

1/2 lb. shredded pork
1/4 lb. shredded bamboo shoot
1/2 lb. bean sprouts, ends removed
1 oz. vermicelli, soaked in lukewarm water for 20 minutes,
   drained, and cut
5 dried mushrooms, soaked and
   shredded

1/2 lb. spring onions, cut into
   2-inch lengths
1/2 tsp. salt
1 tbsp. wine
2 tbsps. soy sauce
1/4 tsp. monosodium glutamate
14 tbsps. oil
3 eggs, lightly beaten with 1/4
   tsp. salt

Method : 1. Heat 5 tbsps. oil and fry meat and spring onions.   2. Heat
5 more tbsps. oil and fry other vegetables and vermicelli.   3. Mix meat,
vegetables, and vermicelli together and add seasonings.   4. Heat 4 tbsps.

oil and scramble eggs, frying them in one piece. 5. Place scrambled eggs on top of meat and vegetables and serve hot.

Note : Unavailable vegetables may be replaced with others or omitted. Spring onions and bean sprouts should not be fried too long or they will become too juicy.

Bean Curd with Sliced Pork and Chili Pepper Sauce

Ingredients :

1/2 lb. lean fresh pork
1/2 lb. bean curd, cut into 8 cubes
1 clove garlic, cut into small pieces
1 tbsp. bean paste (mien chiang in Chinese, miso in Japanese)
1 tbsp. chopped red pepper
3 tbsps. soy sauce
3 green peppers, quartered and seeded

1 small bamboo shoot, sliced
4 inches carrot, sliced and par-boiled
4 dried mushrooms, soaked in water and halved
1/2 tbsp. sugar
1/4 tsp. monosodium glutamate
9 tbsps. oil

Method : 1. Boil pork for 30 minutes, let cool, and slice thin. 2. Heat 3 tbsps. oil and fry bean curd piece by piece until light brown in color. Remove to a plate. 3. Heat 3 more tbsps. oil, fry garlic for 1 minute, and remove to a plate. 4. Mix bean paste, red pepper, and soy sauce in a dish. 5. Heat last 3 tbsps. oil and fry green peppers, bamboo shoot, carrot, and mushrooms. 6. Add bean-paste mixture, garlic, sugar, pork, and monosodium glutamate, mix well, and continue to fry for 5 minutes. Then add fried bean curd and serve hot.

Barbecued Pork

Ingredients :

A

1 lb. lean pork
6 tbsps. soy sauce
1 leek, chopped
4 slices ginger
2 tbsps. wine
1 clove garlic, cracked

B

1 tsp. sugar
1 tbsp. honey
1 tbsp. oil

Method : 1. Cut pork into long strips about 2 inches wide and 2 inches thick. 2. Soak pork in mixture of A ingredients for half a day or overnight. 3. Rub meat with mixture (B) of honey and sugar. 4. After heating oven to correct temperature for roasting, roast pork strips on rack for 35 minutes. Grease rack with 1 tbsp. oil to prevent meat from sticking. Turn strips over once during roasting process. 5. Remove pork from oven and slice. Serve cold.

Note : Soaked pork may be fried in deep oil instead of roasted. Honey may be omitted.

Sweet and Sour Pork

Ingredients :

A

1 lb. loin of pork
1 tbsp. Chinese (or Japanese) wine or sherry
2 tbsps. soy sauce
2 tbsps. flour
1 tbsp. cornstarch
Oil for deep-frying

B

3 green peppers, quartered and seeded
1 round onion (4 oz.), quartered
1 carrot (4 oz.), cut into small wedges and boiled for 8 minutes
1 bamboo shoot (4 oz.), cut into small wedges
2 slices pineapple, each quartered
5 tbsps. oil

C

6 tbsps. sugar
4 tbsps. soy sauce
1 tbsp. wine
2 tbsps. vinegar
4 tbsps. tomato sauce

1 tbsp. cornstarch, mixed with 1/2 cup water

Method : 1. Cut pork into 1 1/2-inch cubes and mix well with other A ingredients except oil. 2. Fry pork in deep oil until crisp and golden brown. Turn out on plate. 3. Heat frying pan, add 5 tbsps. oil, and sauté B ingredients. 4. Mix C ingredients in bowl and add to sautéed B ingredients. 5. When mixture boils up, add cornstarch mixture, stirring constantly. 6. Add fried pork and mix well. Serve hot.

Gold Coin Pork

Ingredients:
1 lb. pork fillet, sliced
3 oz. pork fat, sliced
10 dried mushrooms
Oil for deep-frying

A
4 tbsps. soy sauce
2 tsps. wine
1 tsp. minced ginger
1/2 leek, chopped
2 cloves star aniseed

B
2 tbsps. sugar
1/2 tbsp. sesame oil

Method: 1. Marinate pork, pork fat, and mushrooms in mixture of A ingredients for at least 1 hour. Save A ingredients for use as seasoning. 2. Using a square-shaped skewer or a Japanese chopstick (the *waribashi* type used in restaurants), spear successive pieces of pork, pork fat, and mushroom until skewer is filled. 3. Heat oil and deep-fry the skewered ingredients. 4. Heat the A ingredients used for marinating, adding B ingredients. 5. Remove pork, pork fat, and mushrooms from skewer and dip in heated seasonings (A and B ingredients).

Note: When fried, the skewered pork, pork fat, and mushrooms will have the shape of ancient Chinese coins: round, with a square center hole. For this reason, a square-shaped skewer or chopstick should be used if possible, so that the center hole will not be too small. The skewered ingredients should not be fried too long.

Sliced White Pork

Ingredients:
2 lbs. uncooked pork or bacon
1 onion, cut into small pieces
3 slices ginger

1 clove garlic, ground
4 tbsps. soy sauce

Method: 1. Boil pork with onion and ginger for 40 minutes. Be sure water is deep enough to cover meat. 2. Allow pork to cool; then cut in thin slices. 3. Mix ground garlic with soy sauce and serve as seasoning for dipping pork slices.

Note: If pressure cooker is used, pork should be cooked for only 15 minutes.

Pork

87

Sweet and Sour Meat Balls

Ingredients :

A

1 lb. ground pork
1 stalk leek, chopped
1 tsp. ginger juice
1 tbsp. wine
1 1/2 tbsps. soy sauce
1/2 tsp. salt
1 egg
1/2 tsp. monosodium glutamate
2 tbsps. cornstarch

Oil for deep-frying
1 carrot, sliced and cooked (3/4 cup as sliced)

1/2 cup snow peas, strung and cooked
3 tbsps. oil

B

Sauce:
5 tbsps. sugar
4 tbsps. vinegar
3 tbsps. soy sauce
1/2 tsp. salt
1 tbsp. wine
1/2 cup broth (or water)
1 1/2 tbsps. cornstarch, mixed with 1 cup water

Method : 1. Mix all A ingredients together thoroughly and form into small meat balls with a tablespoon. 2. Heat oil and deep-fry meat balls until done. Remove to a plate. 3. Mix sauce ingredients except corn-starch mixture in a bowl. 4. Heat 3 tbsps. oil and fry carrot slices and snow peas for several minutes. Pour sauce mixture over them and allow it to heat. 5. Add fried meat balls. When mixture boils up again, add cornstarch mixture to thicken. Serve hot.

Note : Ground fish may be substituted for ground pork.

Steamed Gold and Silver Pork

Ingredients :

1/4 lb. sliced pork
6 slices bean curd, each 1/2 inch thick
4 slices boiled ham
5 dried mushrooms
1 leek, cut into 1/4-inch slices

6 slices ginger root
1 tsp. salt
1 tsp. wine
1/2 tsp. monosodium glutamate
Dash pepper
2 tsps. cornstarch

Method : 1. Soak mushrooms in lukewarm water for 15 minutes, remove stems, and cut mushrooms in half. 2. Cut ham slices in half. 3. Rub a little oil on inside of a bowl. Arrange pork and ham slices, mushrooms, and bean curd alternately in the bowl. 4. Sprinkle salt, wine, pepper, leek, and ginger over arranged ingredients. 5. Place bowl in steamer and steam contents for 30 minutes. 6. Loosen edge of contents with a spatula and pour off gravy into a pan. Invert bowl over a platter and remove contents. 7. Heat gravy, adding enough water to make one cupful. Stir in 2 tsps. cornstarch. Add monosodium glutamate and pour hot gravy over steamed ingredients before serving.

Braised Pork with Eggs

Ingredients :

    1 1/2 lbs. pork bacon,
        cut into 1 1/2-inch
        cubes
    3 tbsps. oil
    3 tbsps. wine
    6 tbsps. soy sauce
    1 tbsp. sugar
    1 stalk leek, cut into
        1 1/2-inch lengths
    6 slices ginger
    2 cups water
    4 boiled eggs

Method : 1. Heat oil and fry pork cubes until meat changes color and shrinks. 2. Add wine and soy sauce. Continue to cook until soy sauce is absorbed by meat. Then remove to a deep pan. 3. Add sugar, leek, ginger, and water. Cover tightly and cook over low flame for 1 hour. (If pressure cooker is used, time element will be reduced.) 4. Add boiled eggs and simmer for 30 minutes. 5. Before serving, slice eggs in half. 6. Serve hot in sauce that remains after simmering.

Braised Pork with Quail Eggs

Ingredients :

    1 lb. pork bacon or fillet
    1/2 cup soy sauce
    1 tbsp. wine
    20 quail eggs, boiled and
        shelled
    1 tbsp. flour
    Deep oil for frying eggs
    1 walnut-size piece
        ginger, cracked
    1/2 stalk leek
    1 clove garlic, cracked
    2 cloves aniseed
    2 tbsps. granulated or
        crystal sugar
    Water for boiling pork

Method : 1. Cut pork into bite-size pieces and soak in mixture of soy sauce and wine for 1 hour. 2. Roll boiled quail eggs in flour, deep fry, and remove to a plate. 3. Remove pork from soaking mixture and place in pan with sufficient water to cook (covered) for 40 minutes. Cook pork with ginger, leek, garlic, and aniseed until tender. 4. Add 2 tbsps. sugar. Then add eggs and simmer for 10 minutes. Serve hot.

Braised Pork with Turnips

Ingredients:

1 lb. rump pork	*1 lb. turnips*
1 egg	*2 tbsps. soy sauce*
1/2 tsp. salt	*1/2 tsp. salt*
4 tbsps. flour	*1 tbsp. wine*
Oil for deep-frying	*Water for simmering pork*

Method: 1. Cut pork into bite-size pieces. 2. Mix egg, salt, and flour to form batter. Coat pork with batter and fry in deep oil. Remove to a plate. 3. Peel turnips and cut into bite-size pieces. 4. Place turnips in pan, put fried pork on top, and add seasonings. Then add sufficient water for simmering. 5. Cover with lid and simmer for 1 1/2 hours. Serve hot.

Molded Steamed Bean Curd

Ingredients:

A

1 piece (2 cups) bean curd	*1/2 tsp. wine*
1 egg white, unbeaten	
1/2 tsp. salt	
1/4 tsp. monosodium glutamate	*1 oz. snow peas, strung and parboiled*

B

	1 oz. diced carrots, boiled
1 oz. minced pork	*1 tbsp. sesame oil*
1 egg yolk	*1/2 tsp. salt*
1 tsp. chopped onion	*2 tsps. cornstarch*
1 tsp. ginger juice	*1/2 cup water*
1/2 tsp. salt	*1/4 tsp. monosodium glutamate*

Method: 1. Mix A ingredients thoroughly in a bowl. In another bowl, mix B ingredients thoroughly. 2. Using 12 Chinese porcelain spoons or 12 molds of this size, place 1 1/2 tsps. of A mixture in each. Place 1 tsp. of B mixture on top of this to form a layer. Cover this with another 1 1/2 tsps. of A mixture to form a rounded top. 3. Place filled spoons (or molds) in steamer and steam over strong flame for 15 minutes. 4. Sauté snow peas and diced carrots in 1 tbsp. sesame oil, adding 1/2 tsp. salt. 5. Mix 2 tsps. cornstarch with 1/2 cup water and add to sautéed vegetables, stirring constantly. When mixture boils up, add monosodium glutamate. 6. Unmold steamed bean curd on serving dish, cover with sauce, and serve hot.

Steamed
Meat Balls

Ingredients :
    1 cup glutinous rice
    1 lb. ground pork
    1 egg white
    4 tbsps. chopped leek
    1 tbsp. soy sauce
    1 tsp. salt
    1 tbsp. wine
    1/4 tsp. monosodium
        glutamate

Method : 1. Soak glutinous rice at least 3 hours. Drain.   2. Mix pork thoroughly with all other ingredients and form four large balls.   3. Roll pork balls in glutinous rice until they are heavily covered.   4. Arrange on plate and steam for 40 minutes. Serve hot with soy sauce and mustard.

Stewed Meat Balls
with Cabbage

Ingredients :

A	B
1 lb. pork, finely ground or minced	2 tbsps. soy sauce
1 stalk leek, chopped	2 cups water
1 tsp. minced ginger	3 tbsps. wine
1/2 cup chopped water chestnuts or bamboo shoots (may be omitted)	
1 egg, lightly beaten	1 tbsp. cornstarch, mixed with
1 tbsp. wine	2 tbsps. water
1 tsp. salt	1/2 cup oil for frying
1 tbsp. soy sauce	2 lbs. round or Chinese cabbage

Method : 1. Using chopsticks or a fork, mix A ingredients thoroughly. Wet hands with cornstarch mixture and mold meat mixture into four large balls.   2. Heat oil and fry meat balls to golden brown. Remove to a plate. 3. Separate cabbage leaf by leaf, cut coarsely, and wash.   4. Using same oil as for meat balls, fry cabbage for 2 minutes.   5. Spread cabbage in bottom of pan, place meat balls on top, add mixture B, and simmer for 1 hour.

Note : This dish may be prepared in sufficient quantity for two meals. Flavor of leftover portion will not change during interval. Simply reheat before serving.

Pork

Fried Pork Kidneys with Chili Pepper

Ingredients :

A

2 pork kidneys
1 tbsp. wine
1 tsp. salt
1 tbsp. cornstarch
Oil for deep-frying

B

3 tbsps. oil
1 clove garlic, cracked
2 chili peppers
1 tbsp. soy sauce
1 tbsp. wine
1 tsp. sugar
1 1/2 tsps. vinegar
Dash monosodium glutamate

Method : 1. Cut kidneys in half lengthwise and remove white muscle. Soak kidneys in water for at least 15 minutes. 2. Score each kidney on one side in crisscross pattern. Then slice into bite-size and wash. 3. Dredge with wine, salt, and cornstarch. Then fry in deep oil and remove to a plate. 4. Heat 3 tbsps. oil and brown garlic. Then add fried kidneys and remainder of B seasonings. Serve hot.

Chilled Pork Kidneys

Ingredients :

A	**B**
2 pork kidneys	1 tsp. ginger juice
5 tbsps. chopped leek	1 tsp. sesame oil
1 tsp. ground ginger	1 tbsp. vinegar
1 tbsp. wine	1 tsp. wine
	1 tbsp. soy sauce
	1 tsp. sugar

Method : 1. Cut kidneys in half lengthwise and remove white muscle. Soak kidneys in water for at least 15 minutes. 2. Score each kidney on one side in crisscross pattern. Then slice into bite-size pieces and wash. 3. Bring to a boil sufficient water to cover kidneys. Add chopped leek, ground ginger, and wine to boiling water. Then drop kidneys in and stir briskly. When kidneys change color, remove from heat and drain. 4. Allow kidneys to cool. Then mix with B seasonings and serve cold.

EGGS

Eggs Boiled with Tea Leaves
Egg Roll
Scrambled Eggs with Shredded Pork
Scrambled Eggs with Spinach
Scrambled Egg Yolks
Scrambled Eggs with Shrimp
Eggs with Sweet-sour Sauce
Green Peppers Stuffed with Eggs
Egg Fu Yung
Egg Balls with Ham
Egg and Meat Balls
Pork Omelets
Meat Omelets
Steamed Egg with Clams
Steamed Eggs with Ground Pork
Steamed Quail Eggs
Boiled Eggs with Soy Sauce
Fried Egg with Shark's Fin

HORS D'OEUVRES (2)

Another tempting arrangement of hors d'oeuvres to add sparkle to a cocktail party or to precede the main courses of a full-scale dinner. The nine dishes shown here are varied enough to please an equal number of discriminating palates.

Center: Sliced Cold Chicken (page 36)
Counterclockwise from bottom, left:
Cold Chicken Liver and Giblets (page 36)
Fried Shredded Potatoes (page 110)
Barbecued Pork (page 86)
Cracked Red Radishes
Smoked Fish (page 48)
Boiled Eggs with Soy Sauce (page 103)
Pan-fried Peanuts
Spiced Soy Beans (page 126)

Eggs Boiled with Tea Leaves

Ingredients :

10 eggs	1 tbsp. black pepper
3 tbsps. black tea	5 cloves aniseed
2 tbsps. salt	2 tbsps. soy sauce

Method :   1. Boil eggs for 10 minutes. Soak in cold water and crack shells lightly with a spoon. Do not remove shells.   2. Add tea and seasonings and boil eggs again, this time for 20 minutes.   3 Remove shells. The resulting pattern makes a lovely picture.   4. Slice eggs into quarters and serve.

Note :   This is an excellent item for a picnic.

Egg Roll

Ingredients :

1/2 lb. ground beef or pork	3 tbsps. chopped onion
2 tsps. wine	3 eggs
2 tsps. soy sauce	Dash salt
1 tsp. ginger juice	3 tbsps. flour, mixed with 3 tbsps.
1/4 tsp. salt	water
2 tsps. cornstarch	Oil for deep-frying

Method :   1. Mix ground meat thoroughly with wine, soy sauce, ginger juice, salt, cornstarch, and chopped onion. Divide mixture into 6 portions. 2. Beat eggs, adding dash salt, and fry into 6 egg sheets.   3. Place portion of meat mixture on each egg sheet and roll. Seal with mixture of flour and water. 4. Heat oil, and deep-fry.   5. Drain rolls and then cut each on the bias into 5 pieces.   6. Serve hot with mixture of salt and pepper in separate dish for dipping.

Scrambled Eggs with Shredded Pork

Ingredients:
1/2 lb. pork, shredded
2 stalks leek, shredded
6 eggs, beaten
10 tbsps. oil
4 tbsps. soy sauce
1 tbsp. wine
1/2 tsp. sugar

Method: 1. Heat 6 tbsps. oil, fry beaten eggs slightly, and remove to a plate. 2. Heat 4 tbsps. oil, fry leek for 2 minutes, and add pork. 3. When pork changes color, add half-cooked eggs. 4. Add wine, soy sauce, and sugar. Stir well and serve hot.

Note: This is a tasty dish and simple to make.

Scrambled Eggs with Spinach

Ingredients:

1/2 lb. spinach
5 eggs
8 tbsps. oil

1 1/2 tsps. salt
Dash monosodium glutamate

Method: 1. Thoroughly wash spinach and cut into 3 sections. 2. Beat eggs lightly, adding 1/2 tsp. salt. 3. Heat 4 tbsps. oil and scramble eggs. Remove to a plate. 4. Heat remaining 4 tbsps. oil and fry spinach until tender, adding 1 tsp. salt. 5. Add scrambled eggs to spinach and mix. Serve hot.

Scrambled Egg Yolks

Ingredients:

6 egg yolks
2 cups chicken or meat soup, cold
5 tbsps. chopped ham
1/2 cup chopped bamboo shoot
1 tbsp. wine

1 tsp. salt
2 tbsps. cornstarch, mixed with
2 tbsps. water
5 tbsps. oil

Method: 1. Beat egg yolks and mix with cold soup. Add 3 tbsps. chopped ham, all of chopped bamboo shoot, wine, salt, and cornstarch mixture. Beat again until well-mixed. 2. Heat 5 tbsps. oil, add mixture, and stir constantly until it thickens. 3. Sprinkle remaining 2 tbsps. chopped ham over eggs as a garnish.

Note: In order that both egg yolks and egg whites may be used, prepare this dish along with another that calls for egg whites only, for example, Fried Prawns with Egg White Batter, Velvet Chicken and Sweet Corn Soup, Bird's Nest Soup with Flowing Egg White, or Chicken Fu Yung.

Scrambled Eggs with Shrimp

Ingredients:
1/2 lb. shrimp
1 tsp. wine
1 tsp. ginger juice
1 tsp. cornstarch
8 tbsps. oil
6 eggs
1 tsp. salt
1/4 tsp. monosodium
   glutamate

Method: 1. Shell and clean shrimp, removing black line. 2. Grind ginger and squeeze out juice. 3. Dredge shrimp with wine, ginger juice, and cornstarch. 4. Heat 3 tbsps. oil, fry shrimp until color changes, remove from pan, and allow to cool. 5. Beat eggs lightly and mix with shrimp, adding salt and monosodium glutamate. 6. Heat another 5 tbsps. oil until very hot; then fry shrimp-and-egg mixture. Turn mixture over when one side is cooked and cook until other side turns light brown. Serve hot.

Eggs with Sweet-sour Sauce

Ingredients:

6 eggs	1/2 tbsp. vinegar
3 tbsps. oil (or more)	1/2 tbsp. sugar
1 tbsp. soy sauce	1/8 tsp. monosodium glutamate

Method: 1. Heat 1 1/2 tbsps. oil and fry eggs individually, first breaking each into a small bowl. When egg has set, fold over in half-moon shape, seal edge tightly, and remove to a plate. Add oil as needed during frying. 2. Place eggs in pan again, adding soy sauce, vinegar, sugar, and monosodium glutamate. Bring to a boil, remove from pan, and serve hot.

Green Peppers Stuffed with Eggs

Ingredients:

4 medium green peppers	1 tsp. ginger juice
8 hard-boiled eggs, chopped	1 tsp. salt
1/4 lb. crab meat, boned and chopped	1/6 tsp. monosodium glutamate
	2 tbsps. sesame oil

Method: 1. Cut green peppers in half lengthwise and remove seeds. 2. Mix chopped egg and crab meat with seasonings and stuff green pepper halves with mixture. 3. Steam for 15 minutes, sprinkle with sesame oil, and serve hot.

Egg Fu Yung

Ingredients:

1/2 lb. canned crab meat
1 tsp. minced ginger
1 tbsp. wine
2 dried mushrooms, soaked
  and shredded
6 slices bamboo shoot,
  shredded
1/2 stalk leek, shredded
2 tbsps. green peas
6 eggs
1 1/2 tsps. salt
9 tbsps. oil
1 cup soup stock
2 tbsps. soy sauce
1 tbsp. cornstarch, mixed
  with 1 tbsp. water

Method: 1. Remove bone from crab meat, break meat into fragments, and mix with ginger and wine. 2. Beat eggs lightly and add crab meat and salt. 3. Heat 7 tbsps. oil and fry crab-and-egg mixture in size of a 9-inch omelet or in smaller omelets for individual servings. Fry on both sides. 4. Heat remaining 2 tbsps. oil and fry mushrooms, bamboo shoot, and leek. Add soy sauce, green peas, and soup stock to form sauce. When sauce boils up, thicken with cornstarch mixture. 5. Pour sauce over omelet and serve hot.

Egg Balls with Ham

Ingredients:

1/2 lb. ham, chopped
1 tbsp. chopped onion
1/4 tsp. salt
Dash pepper
3 eggs, beaten lightly

2 tbsps. flour (or more)
3 slices bread, trimmed and diced
1 cup dry vermicelli cut into
  1/2-inch lengths
Oil for deep-frying

Method: 1. Mix chopped ham, onion, salt, pepper, eggs, and diced bread together, adding about 2 tbsps. flour or enough to make a thick paste. 2. Using a teaspoon, form mixture into about 30 balls. 3. Roll balls in cut dry vermicelli. 4. Heat oil and deep-fry balls until golden brown. The fried vermicelli will curl up to make the balls resemble chestnut burrs. Serve hot.

Egg and Meat Balls

Ingredients :
  6 hard-boiled eggs
  3/4 lb. ground meat (beef or pork)
  3/4 tsp. salt
  1 tbsp. cornstarch, mixed with
    3 tbsps. water
  1 tsp. ginger juice
  2 tsps. wine
  Oil for deep-frying
  Sauce:
  1 tsp. salt
  2 tbsps. soy sauce
  1 tsp. sugar
  1 tbsp. cornstarch
  1 cup juice from egg-meat balls
    after steaming

Method : 1. Cut hard-boiled eggs in half. Sprinkle top of each with flour
and cut small slice off bottom to prevent halves from rolling on plate.
2. Mix ground meat with salt, cornstarch mixture, ginger juice, and wine.
Form into 12 thick patties to fit tops of egg-halves. 3. Place one patty on
top of each egg-half and steam for 10 minutes. 4. Heat oil and deep-fry
egg-meat balls. Remove to serving dish. 5. Heat sauce ingredients and
pour over egg-meat balls. Serve hot.

Pork Omelets

Ingredients :
  4 eggs, lightly beaten   Sauce:
  1/2 cup cooked pork, diced small 1 tbsp. soy sauce
  3/4 tsp. salt   1 tsp. sugar
  2 tbsps. chopped leek   1 cup broth
  1/4 tsp. monosodium glutamate   1 tbsp. cornstarch
  1/4 cup broth or water   1/2 tsp. salt
  3 tbsps. oil   1/6 tsp. monosodium glutamate

Method : 1. Mix beaten eggs with pork, salt, leek, monosodium glutamate,
and broth. Divide mixture into 4 portions and fry in 3 tbsps. oil. Fold over
and fry until done. Remove to a plate. 2. Mix all sauce ingredients except
cornstarch and bring to a boil. Add cornstarch for thickening. 3. Pour
sauce over omelets and serve hot.

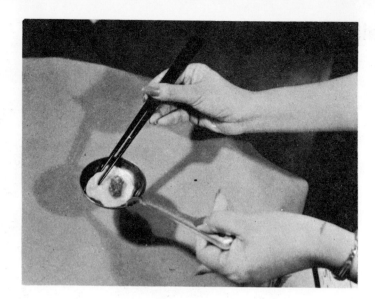

Meat Omelets

Ingredients :

A

2 or 3 eggs, lightly beaten
1/4 lb. ground meat
2 tbsps. soy sauce
1/2 tsp. salt
2 tbsps. chopped onion
1 tsp. ginger juice

1 bunch spinach (1/2 lb.)
1 1/2 tsps. salt
3 tbsps. oil

B

1 tbsp. soy sauce
1/2 tsp. salt
2 cups broth
1 tbsp. cornstarch

Method : 1. Mix meat and seasonings thoroughly. 2. Grease ladle or small frying pan and heat. When hot, pour in 1 tsp. of beaten egg and allow to set slightly. 2. Then place small quantity of meat mixture on egg, fold over in half-moon shape, and fry. Continue making omelets until all of egg has been used. 4. Heat 3 tbsps. oil, fry spinach, and add salt. 5. Boil omelets in broth for about 10 minutes, adding soy sauce and salt and thickening with cornstarch (B ingredients). 6. Pour broth and omelets over fried spinach and serve hot.

Steamed Egg with Clams

Ingredients :
12 clams
2 eggs
1 tsp. salt
2 tsps. wine
1/2 tsp. sugar
2 cups water
1/2 tsp. monosodium
    glutamate
A few drops sesame oil
A few drops soy sauce

Method : 1. Soak clams in their shells in salted water for 15 minutes so that they will eject any remaining grit or sand. Use clams in their shells. 2. Beat eggs and add salt, wine, sugar, water, monosodium glutamate, and clams. 3. Steam mixture for 10 minutes over boiling water. 4. Before serving, sprinkle with sesame oil and soy sauce.

Steamed Eggs with Ground Pork

Ingredients:
    3 oz. ground pork
    1 tsp. wine
    1 tbsp. soy sauce
    2 eggs
    1 tsp. ginger juice
    1 tsp. salt
    1 cup broth or water
    1 tsp. sesame oil
    1 tsp. soy sauce

Method: 1. Mix ground pork with wine and soy sauce. 2. Beat eggs and add ginger juice, salt, broth (or water), and meat. Mix well and place in a deep dish. 3. Steam for 20 minutes or until eggs are set. 4. Sprinkle with 1 tsp. sesame oil and 1 tsp. soy sauce and serve hot.

Steamed Quail Eggs

Ingredients:

1/4 lb. ground pork	1/4 tsp. cornstarch
1/4 tsp. salt	14 quail eggs
1 tsp. wine	

Method: 1. Mix ground pork, salt, wine, and cornstarch thoroughly. 2. Using 14 Chinese porcelain spoons or small wine cups as dishes, grease each of these and place 1/2 tsp. of the meat mixture in it. 3. Break a quail egg over mixture in each spoon and sprinkle lightly with salt. 4. Place spoons in steamer and steam for 10 minutes. 5. Loosen edges of steamed eggs with spatula, remove to a plate, and garnish with minced parsley and slivers of soaked (or cooked) dry mushroom. 6. Serve either hot or cold.

Boiled Eggs with Soy Sauce

Ingredients:
    5 eggs
    4 tbsps. soy sauce
    1 tsp. sugar
    1 tsp. sesame oil
    4 tbsps. water

Method: 1. Boil eggs for 5 minutes. Soak in cold water and remove shells. 2. Heat soy sauce, sugar, sesame oil, and 4 tbsps. water. Simmer eggs in this mixture for 5 minutes over low flame. Then allow them to soak in mixture for 30 minutes. Turn eggs in mixture until evenly colored. 3. Cut each egg into quarters and serve cold.

Note: This item is excellent as an hors d'œuvre.

Fried Egg with Shark's Fin

Ingredients:

1 oz. refined shark's fin   1 tsp. ginger juice
1 stalk leek   1 1/2 tsps. salt
3 slices ginger   1/2 tsp. sugar
4 eggs   8 tbsps. oil
1 tbsp. wine

Method: 1. Soak refined shark's fin overnight. Rinse in cold water and boil for 1 hour with leek and ginger. (A pinch of baking soda may be added during boiling.) 2. Rinse and drain shark's fin 3 times after boiling. 3. Beat eggs; add shark's fin and seasonings. 4. Heat 8 tbsps. oil and fry mixture until eggs are set. Serve hot.

VEGETABLES AND SALADS

Fried Bamboo Shoots with Chili Sauce
Fried Bamboo Shoots with Mustard Greens
Fried Cabbage with Fresh Mushrooms
Fried Lettuce
Fried Shredded Potatoes
Fried Lima Beans
Fried Bean Sprouts with Green Peppers
Fried Shredded Turnips
Fried Spinach
Fried Mixed Vegetables
Fried Vermicelli with Vegetables
Pressed Bean Curd with Assorted Meat
Green Peppers Stuffed with Carrots
Vegetable Rolls
Potato "Hamburgers"
Braised Bamboo Shoots with Mushrooms
Braised Pumpkin
Braised Lima Beans
Braised Bean Curd
Braised Mushrooms
Creamed Bamboo Shoots
Creamed Chinese Cabbage
Vinegar Sautéed Cabbage
Bean Curd Paper Sheet Rolls
Sweet and Sour Mustard Greens
Steamed Eggplants with Egg
Chilled Eggplants
Chilled Sweet and Sour Cucumbers
Cucumber and Chicken with Chili Pepper Sauce
Chilled Cucumbers
Chilled Cucumbers and Red Radishes
Sweet and Sour Vegetable Salad
Meat and Vegetable Salad
Chopped Spinach Salad
Pork, Spinach, and Tomato Salad
Turnip Salad

Jellyfish with Turnips
Jellyfish with Chicken and Cucumber
Chinese Pickles
Crab Meat with Cucumber
Sliced Lotus Root
Sweet and Sour Chinese Cabbage Rolls
Spiced Soy Beans

COLOR AND COOLNESS FOR
HOT DAYS

The rainbow effect of cold shredded vegetables and meat is charmingly complemented by the intriguing brown pattern of eggs that have been boiled with tea leaves. Ingredients used in making the salad are shown in several stages of preparation. The two types of vermicelli, either of which may be used in this dish, are *yang fên* (made from seaweed) at lower right and *fên ssŭ* (made from green beans) at left center. On the cutting board are cucumber, ham, and shredded egg sheet. The bowl contains sauce for dressing.

Center: Meat and Vegetable Salad (page 122)

Lower left: Eggs Boiled with Tea Leaves (page 97)

Fried Bamboo Shoots with Chili Sauce

Ingredients:

2 1/2 lbs. fresh bamboo shoot
Oil for deep-frying
3 tbsps. oil
2 tsps. chili sauce

1 tbsp. soy sauce
1 tsp. sugar
Dash monosodium glutamate

Method: 1. Boil bamboo shoot for 25 minutes, drain, and cut into thin bias strips. 2. Heat oil for deep-frying and fry bamboo strips to golden brown. Remove to a plate. 3. Heat 3 tbsps. oil and add chili sauce. When mixture is hot, add bamboo, soy sauce, sugar, and monosodium glutamate. Stir for several minutes, remove to serving dish, and serve hot.

Fried Bamboo Shoots with Mustard Greens

Ingredients:

1 1/2 lbs. fresh bamboo shoot
(or 3/4 lb. canned bamboo shoot)
1/4 lb. fresh mustard greens
(leaves only)

1 tsp. sugar
1/2 tsp. salt
Oil for deep-frying

Method: 1. Peel fresh bamboo shoot, cook in boiling water for 25 minutes, drain, and cut into thin diagonal strips. 2. Heat deep oil and fry bamboo shoot to a golden brown. Drain, place in serving dish, and mix with 1 tsp. sugar and 1/2 tsp. salt. 3. Wash mustard leaves, drain, and wipe. Heat deep oil again and fry leaves until they become very crisp. Guard against splashing oil when deep-frying leaves; use lid to cover until splashing stops. 4. Remove fried leaves from oil to serving dish, sprinkle lightly with sugar and salt, and place fried bamboo shoot on top. Serve hot.

Fried Cabbage with Fresh Mushrooms

Ingredients:

1/2 lb. fresh mushrooms
1/2 lb. round cabbage, cored and trimmed
6 tbsps. oil

2 tsps. salt
1 tsp. sugar
1 tsp. wine
Dash monosodium glutamate

Method: 1. Wash mushrooms, slice, and soak them in salt water for about 20 minutes. 2. Cut cabbage into small sections about 2 inches square and wash. 3. Heat oil and fry mushrooms and cabbage until tender. Then add seasonings, mix well, and serve hot.

Note: Fresh mushrooms are called *hsiang ku* in Chinese and *matsutake* in Japanese. They are products of autumn in China and Japan.

Fried Lettuce

Ingredients:
1 lb. leaf lettuce
1 tsp. salt
1 clove garlic, crushed

1/6 tsp. monosodium glutamate
5 tbsps. oil

Method: 1. Wash lettuce and drain. 2. Heat oil, brown crushed garlic, add lettuce, salt, and monsodium glutamate; fry for 1 minute. Serve hot when leaves turn brighter green.

Fried Shredded Potatoes

Ingredients:
4 potatoes, shredded
1/2 tsp. salt

Oil for deep-frying

Method: 1. Peel potatoes, shred, and soak in water for 10 minutes. 2. Drain potatoes on cheesecloth. 3. Fry 1/4 of potatoes at a time in deep oil until color turns light brown. Stir with chopsticks to prevent potatoes from sticking together. Sprinkle with salt while still hot.

Note: This dish may be served as one of those used for filling Pancake Rolls (see page 133).

Fried Lima Beans

Ingredients:
1 lb. shelled fresh lima beans (or 4 lbs. unshelled)
5 tbsps. oil
3 tbsps. sugar
1 tbsp. salt
1/2 cup water
1/4 tsp. monosodium glutamate

Method: 1. Heat oil and fry lima beans until color becomes greener. 2. Add water and seasonings and boil for 5 minutes over high flame. Serve hot or cold.

Fried Bean Sprouts with Green Peppers

Ingredients :
- *1 lb. bean sprouts*
- *3 green peppers*
- *5 tbsps. oil*
- *2 tbsps. wine*
- *1 tsp. salt*
- *1/4 tsp. monosodium glutamate*

Method : 1. Remove heads and tails of bean sprouts and soak sprouts in water until ready to use. Drain before using. 2. Wash, seed, and shred green peppers. 3. Heat 5 tbsps. oil and fry bean sprouts and shredded green peppers. Add wine, salt, and monosodium glutamate. Serve hot.

Note : Do not overfry bean sprouts.

Fried Shredded Turnips

Ingredients :

1 lb. turnips, shredded	*1/2 tsp. sugar*
3 tbsps. oil	*1 cup water*
1/2 tsp. salt	*Dash monosodium glutamate*
1 tbsp. soy sauce	

Method : 1. Peel and shred turnips. 2. Heat oil and fry turnips. Add seasonings and water and simmer for 10 minutes. Serve either hot or cold.

Fried Spinach

Ingredients :

1 lb. spinach	*1 tsp. salt*
3 tbsps. oil	

Method : 1. Wash spinach and drain. Cut into 2 or 3 sections. 2. Heat oil and fry spinach, adding salt. Stir over strong flame for 5 minutes. Serve hot.

Fried Mixed Vegetables

Ingredients :

8 oz. round cabbage, cut into small pieces

5 dried mushrooms, soaked, stemmed, and halved

3 oz. bamboo shoot, cut into 1 1/2 inch strips

1 oz. snow peas, strung and boiled

3 inches carrot, sliced and boiled

1 cucumber, sliced

5 tbsps. chicken oil (or salad oil)

5 tbsps. soup stock

1 tsp. salt

1 tsp. sugar

2 tsps. soy sauce

1/2 tsp. monosodium glutamate

Method : 1. Prepare vegetable ingredients as indicated above. Bamboo shoot should be sliced into thin strips. Then make slits in edge of each strip so that it looks like a comb. 2. Heat 5 tbsps. oil and fry cabbage first. Then add bamboo and other vegetable ingredients and fry mixture for 5 minutes. 3. Add soup stock and seasonings and mix. Do not cook too long. This dish may be served either hot or cold.

Fried Vermicelli with Vegetables

Ingredients :

1 oz. vermicelli (fên ssǔ *in* Chinese, harusame *in* Japanese)

6 dried mushrooms (1 cup as soaked and shredded)

4 small bamboo shoots (1 cup as shredded)

4 pieces fried bean curd (2 cups as shredded)

1/2 lb. green peppers (2 cups as shredded)

7 tbsps. oil

1 tsp. salt

3 tbsps. soy sauce

1/2 tbsp. sugar

Dash monosodium glutamate

Method : 1. Soak vermicelli in hot water for at least 5 minutes, drain, and cut into 3-inch lengths. 2. Prepare vegetable ingredients as instructed above. 3. Heat 7 tbsps. oil and sauté vegetable ingredients. 4. When these become tender, add vermicelli and seasonings. This dish may be served hot or cold.

Note : Fried bean curd is *you tou fu* in Chinese, *abura-age* in Japanese. This ingredient may be omitted if unavailable.

Pressed Bean Curd with Assorted Meat

Ingredients :

2 cakes bean curd (1 lb.)

1/2 cup cooked chicken meat

1/2 cup cooked ham

1/2 cup shrimp

4 cups broth

1 tbsp. wine

2 tsps. salt

Method : 1. Place bean curd in boiling water to which 2 tsps. salt have been added. 2. When bean curd floats, remove from water, wrap in cheesecloth, and place between 2 wooden boards. Place weight on top to press.

out liquid and allow to stand for about 3 hours, or until bean curd becomes solid. 3. Shred hardened bean curd, chicken meat, and ham. 4. Shell shrimp and remove black lines. 5. Heat broth and add all other ingredients and seasonings. Boil for 20 minutes and serve hot.

Note : Bamboo shoot and mushroom may be added to this dish.

Green Peppers Stuffed with Carrots

Ingredients :
    10 medium green peppers
    3 cups shredded carrots
    1 cup shredded onion
    4 tbsps. oil
    6 tbsps. tomato catsup
    1 tbsp. sugar
    1 tsp. salt
    Dash pepper
    1/4 tsp. monosodium glutamate
    1 cup water

Method : 1. Parboil green peppers, rinse in cold water, and drain. 2. Cut off tops of peppers and remove seeds. 3. Heat 4 tbsps. oil and sauté shredded carrot and onion. Add seasonings. 4. Stuff peppers with mixture, place in pan, add water, and simmer for 20 minutes or until tender. Serve hot.

Vegetable Rolls

Ingredients :
    8 bean curd paper sheets
    1 cup bean curd
    1/4 lb. chopped spinach
        (or other greens)
    4 dry mushrooms, soaked
        and chopped
    1/2 tsp. salt
    1/2 tsp. wine
    1/2 tsp. sesame oil
    3 tbsps. oil
    4 tbsps. broth
    2 tsps. soy sauce

Method : 1. Soak bean curd paper sheets for 1 minute or until soft enough to fold. 2. Mash bean curd and mix with spinach, mushrooms, bamboo shoot, salt, wine, and sesame oil. 3. Using bean curd paper sheets for wrapping, place 1 1/2 tbsps. of mixture on each and form rolls by folding bottom edge up, left and right edges over, and rolling toward top. 4. Heat 3 tbsps. oil and fry rolls on both sides. Add broth and soy sauce and simmer for 10 minutes or until all liquid is absorbed. Serve hot.

Vegetables &
Salads

Potato "Hamburgers"

Ingredients :

1 1/2 lbs. potatoes
4 dried mushrooms,
  soaked in lukewarm
  water (save juice)
2 tbsps. soy sauce
3 tbsps. juice from
  soaked mushrooms
1/2 tbsp. salt
1/2 tsp. monosodium
  glutamate
1/2 cup flour (or more)
6 tbsps. oil
1 small bamboo shoot,
  sliced
1/2 cup green soy beans
  or green peas
1 cup water
1/2 tsp. salt

Method : 1. Peel and boil potatoes. Drain and mash, adding soy sauce, juice from mushrooms, salt, and monosodium glutamate. 2. Heat mixture and add flour. Stir and cook until mixture thickens. 3. Form into 4 large cakes like hamburgers. 4. Heat 4 tbsps. oil and fry potato "hamburgers" on both sides to light brown. Remove to a plate. 5. Heat 2 tbsps. oil and sauté bamboo shoot, mushrooms, and peas. Add water and salt. 6. Add "hamburgers" and boil for 15 minutes or until liquid evaporates.

Braised Bamboo Shoots with Mushrooms

Ingredients :

1/2 lb. canned bamboo shoot	4 tbsps. soy sauce
8 dried mushrooms	2 tbsps. sugar
5 tbsps. oil	1/4 tsp. monosodium glutamate
1 tbsp. wine	6 tbsps. water

Method : 1. Cut bamboo shoot into cubes. 2. Soak mushrooms in hot water for 10 minutes. Remove stems. If large mushrooms are used, halve them. 3. Heat oil and fry bamboo shoot and mushrooms. Add all seasonings and water. Cover with lid and simmer for 20 minutes until liquid dries up. Serve hot.

Note : If fresh bamboo shoot is used, peel shoots, halve them, and boil them for 30 minutes with 2 red peppers.

Braised Pumpkin

Ingredients :

1 lb. pumpkin	*1/2 tsp. salt*
4 tbsps. oil	*1/4 tsp. sugar*
1/2 stalk leek, chopped	*1/2 cup water*

Method : 1. Peel pumpkin and remove seeds. Cut into 2-inch squares. 2. Heat 4 tbsps. oil and fry pumpkin. Add leek, salt, sugar, and water. Simmer for 15 minutes and serve hot.

Braised Lima Beans

Ingredients :

A

2 *cups shelled lima beans (skins also removed)*

1 *cup bamboo shoot, cut into squares*

1 *cup canned champignon mushrooms, cut into halves*

B

1 *cup sliced chicken fillet*
1 *tsp. wine*
1 *tsp. cornstarch*
1/4 *tsp. salt*
3 *tbsps. oil*

C

2 *tsps. salt*
1/2 *tsp. sugar*
1 *tbsp. wine*
1/4 *tsp. monosodium glutamate*

5 *cups broth*
2 1/2 *tbsps. cornstarch, mixed with 2 1/2 tbsps. water*

Method : 1. Dredge chicken fillet with wine, cornstarch, and salt. Heat 3 tbsps. oil and sauté chicken fillet. Remove to a plate. 2. Heat 5 cups broth, add A ingredients, and bring to a boil. 3. Add C ingredients (seasonings) and chicken fillet. 4. Thicken with cornstarch mixture and serve hot.

Braised Bean Curd

Ingredients:
- 2 cakes bean curd
- 2 tbsps. dried shrimp, soaked and chopped
- 4 tbsps. flour
- 2 eggs
- 1/2 tsp. salt
- 9 tbsps. oil
- 2 tbsps. chopped leek
- 1 1/2 cups broth
- 2 tsps. soy sauce
- 1 tsp. salt
- 1 1/2 tbsps. wine
- 1 1/2 tsps. cornstarch, mixed with 3 tbsps. water

Method: 1. Wrap bean curd in cheesecloth and press gently to drain off liquid. Cut each cake into 8 square pieces. 2. Mix flour, eggs, and salt to form batter. 3. Heat 6 tbsps. oil. Coat bean curd squares with batter and fry on both sides to light brown. Remove to a plate. 4. Heat 3 tbsps. oil and brown leek and shrimp. Add bean curd, broth, and seasonings. 5. Thicken with cornstarch mixture and serve hot.

Braised Mushrooms

Ingredients:
- 1/4 lb. (about 20) dried mushrooms
- 5 tbsps. oil
- 1 1/2 tbsps. sugar
- 2 tbsps. soy sauce
- 1 tbsp. sesame oil
- 1/2 cup broth or water
- Dash monosodium glutamate

Method: 1. Soak mushrooms in lukewarm water for 20 to 30 minutes and remove stems. 2. Heat 5 tbsps. oil and fry mushrooms for several minutes. 3. Add sugar, soy sauce, and broth; cover; and simmer for 25 minutes. 4. Add sesame oil and monosodium glutamate before serving. 5. Serve either hot or cold.

Note: This dish, served cold, goes excellently as an hors d'œuvre. If it is used for this purpose, the mushrooms should be sliced thin before serving.

Creamed Bamboo Shoots

Ingredients :

3 lbs. fresh bamboo shoots (or 1 1/2 lbs. canned)
3 tbsps. oil
1 cup water
1/2 cup evaporated milk

1 tsp. cornstarch, mixed with 1 tbsp. water
1 tsp. salt
1 tbsp. chopped boiled ham
1 tbsp. chopped cooked (or fried) mushroom

Method : 1. Peel fresh bamboo shoots, cut off tough parts, and cut shoots into small slices.   2. Heat 3 tbsps. oil and fry bamboo. Add 1 cup water and cook for 10 minutes.   Then add milk, cornstarch mixture and salt. 3. Place in serving dish and sprinkle with chopped ham and mushroom. Serve hot.

Creamed Chinese Cabbage

Ingredients :

1 lb. Chinese cabbage
3 tbsps. chicken oil (rendered from chicken fat)
1 cup broth or water
1/2 cup evaporated milk
1 tsp. salt

1/4 tsp. monosodium glutamate
1 tbsp. cornstarch, mixed with 3 tbsps. water
1 tbsp. chopped boiled ham
4 mushrooms, cooked (or fried) and diced

Method : 1. Cut cabbage into small sections, boil until tender, and drain. 2. Heat 3 tbsps. chicken oil and sauté cabbage.   3. Add broth, milk, salt, and monosodium glutamate and bring to a boil.   4. Add cornstarch mixture and stir well.   5. Remove to serving dish and sprinkle with chopped ham and mushroom. Serve hot.

Vegetables &
Salads

117

Vinegar Sautéed Cabbage

Ingredients :

1 lb. round cabbage	3 red peppers, chopped
4 tbsps. oil	1/2 tsp. salt
2 tbsps. vinegar	Dash monosodium glutamate
1 tbsp. soy sauce	1 tsp. cornstarch, mixed with
2 tbsps. sugar	2 tsps. water
1 clove garlic, cracked	

Method : 1. Wash and cut cabbage into triangle shapes about 2 inches thick. 2. Heat oil, add garlic and red pepper, and fry for 2 minutes. 3. Add cabbage and fry over very strong flame, stirring constantly. 4. Add remaining seasonings and continue to stir over strong flame for another 2 minutes. Add cornstarch mixture and serve hot.

Bean Curd Paper Sheet Rolls

Ingredients :

3 rolls dried bean curd (tou fu pei chüan *in Chinese,* yuba *in Japanese*)
4 1/4 tbsps. soy sauce
1 1/2 tbsps. sugar
1 tbsp. wine
1/2 tsp. monosodium glutamate
1/2 cup water

Method : 1. Cut bean curd rolls into 1-inch lengths. 2. Mix soy sauce, sugar, wine, and water and simmer bean curd rolls in this mixture for 20 minutes. 3. Add monosodium glutamate, chill, and serve cold.

Note : If bean curd rolls cannot be obtained, use sheets of dried bean curd to form rolls—5 sheets per roll.

Sweet and Sour Mustard Greens

Ingredients :

1/2 lb. mustard greens	1 tbsp. soy sauce
1/2 tsp. salt	1 1/2 tbsps. vinegar
3 tbsps. oil	2 tbsps. cornstarch, mixed with
2 tbsps. sugar	5 tbsps. water

Method : 1. Cut mustard greens into sections. 2. Heat 3 tbsps. oil and fry mustard greens, adding 1/2 tsp. salt. 3. When mustard greens become tender, add sugar, soy sauce, and vinegar. 4. Pour in cornstarch mixture, stir quickly, and serve hot.

Steamed Eggplants with Egg

Ingredients:
- 8 small eggplants
- 2 eggs
- 3 tbsps. chopped leek
- 3 tbsps. soy sauce
- 1 tbsp. sugar
- 4 tbsps. oil

Method: 1. Wash and stem eggplants. Steam until tender (15 to 20 minutes). 2. Beat eggs and add chopped leek, soy sauce, and sugar. Mix well. 3. Heat 4 tbsps. oil and sauté egg mixture. Break it into small pieces when it sets. 4. Tear eggplants lengthwise in small pieces. Arrange pieces in circle on a plate and place fried egg mixture in middle. Serve hot.

Chilled Eggplants

Ingredients:
- 1 lb. eggplants (about 5)
- 1 tbsp. soy sauce
- 1 tbsp. sesame oil
- 1 tbsp. sugar
- 1 tsp. salt
- 1/2 tsp. ground ginger root or prepared ground ginger
- 1/4 tsp. monosodium glutamate

Method: 1. Remove stems from eggplants and place eggplants in cold water to prevent discoloration. 2. Steam whole eggplants until tender (15 or 20 minutes). 3. Tear each eggplant lengthwise from top to bottom into quarters. (It is easier to tear than to cut, and tearing prevents mashing.) 4. Mix all remaining ingredients to make sauce. Pour sauce over eggplants and chill before serving.

Vegetables &
Salads

119

Chilled Sweet and Sour Cucumbers

Ingredients :
    9 cucumbers (1 1/2 lbs.)
    2 1/2 tsps. salt
    2 tsps. sugar
    2 dried mushrooms, soaked
        and shredded
    2 red peppers, shredded
    4 slices ginger, shredded
    2 tbsps. sesame oil
Sauce:
    2 tbsps. sugar
    2 tbsps. vinegar
    1 tbsp. cornstarch, mixed
        with 5 tbsps. water

Method : 1. Cut cucumbers into pieces 2 inches long; then cut each piece into 4. Remove seeds and use outer meat and skin only. 2. Sprinkle cucumbers with 2 tsps. salt and let stand for 1 hour. 3. Dip cucumbers in boiling water, drain, and sprinkle with 1/2 tsp. salt and 2 tsps. sugar. Allow seasonings to be absorbed. 4. Heat 2 tbsps. sesame oil in pan and fry mushrooms, red peppers, and ginger. Add sauce seasonings and cornstarch mixture. 5. Mix sauce with cucumbers and chill mixture in refrigerator before serving.

Cucumber and Chicken with Chili Pepper Sauce

Ingredients :

1/2 spring chicken (about 1 lb.)	1 tsp. sugar
3 cucumbers, sliced and shredded	3 tbsps. soy sauce
1 tsp. minced ginger root	3 tbsps. vinegar
5 tbsps. chopped leek	2 tbsps. sesame oil
Sauce:	2 tbsps. red pepper oil or 1/2 tsp.
4 tbsps. white sesame seeds, toasted	tabasco
(without oil) and ground	Dash monosodium glutamate

Method : 1. Boil chicken for about 30 minutes. When cold, shred it. 2. Slice cucumbers and cut into shreds. 3. Mix chicken and cucumbers, arrange on plate, and sprinkle with chopped leek and minced ginger. 4. Prepare sauce by mixing ingredients and pour over chicken and cucumbers before serving.

Note : Use chicken skin as well as meat, since this increases the flavor. This is a cold dish and should be prepared in advance. Sauce can be kept in separate dish until time for serving.

Chilled Cucumbers

Ingredients :
    3 cucumbers   *1 tbsp. sesame oil*
    3 tbsps. soy sauce   *1/6 tsp. monosodium glutamate*

Method :   1. Wash cucumbers with small amount of salt.   2. Remove ends and crack cucumbers with back of heavy knife. Cut into 2 1/2-inch lengths. 3. Soak for 10 minutes in mixture of soy sauce, sesame oil, and monosodium glutamate. Serve chilled.

Chilled Cucumbers and Red Radishes

Ingredients :
    5 small cucumbers   *1 tsp. salt*
    15 red radishes   *3 tbsps. vinegar*
    1 tbsp. soy sauce   *5 tbsps. oil*

Method :   1. Wash and cut cucumbers into thirds. Then cut each third lengthwise into quarters.   2. Wash red radishes and crack them with the back of a heavy knife.   3. Heat 5 tbsps. oil and fry cucumbers and radishes. 4. Add seasonings, stir briskly, and remove from fire.   5. Chill for at least 1 hour before serving.

Sweet and Sour Vegetable Salad

Ingredients:

3 cucumbers	4 tbsps. sugar
1/2 lb. cabbage	1/2 tsp. salt
5 green peppers (or equal quantity round red radishes)	2 tbsps. soy sauce
	3 tbsps. vinegar
3 tbsps. oil	1/4 tsp. monosodium glutamate

Method: 1. Slice cucumbers lengthwise into quarters; then cut each quarter into 3 pieces. 2. Cut cabbage into rough squares. 3. Quarter and seed green peppers. 4. Heat 3 tbsps. oil, fry all vegetable ingredients over strong flame, and add seasonings. 5. Chill salad in refrigerator for at least one hour.

Meat and Vegetable Salad

Ingredients:

2 oz. vermicelli (yang fên in Chinese, ito ganten in Japanese)
4 cucumbers (about 1 lb.), shredded
1/4 lb. chicken fillet (or pork), shredded
3 slices ham, shredded
2 eggs
Sauce:
6 tbsps. soy sauce
1 tsp. ground mustard
3 tbsps. vinegar
1 tsp. sugar
3 tbsps. sesame oil
Dash monosodium glutamate

Method: 1. Wash vermicelli and soak it for 20 minutes in lukewarm water. Then drain and cut into 3-inch sections. 2. Clean cucumbers, removing seedy parts, and shred. 3. Cook chicken fillet and shred. 4. Beat eggs well, fry in 3 or 4 thin egg sheets, and shred. 5. Shred ham. 6. Arrange all ingredients in sections on a platter. Chill. 7. Mix sauce ingredients in bowl. At table, pour sauce over salad and stir ingredients together before serving.

Note: Green bean vermicelli (*fên ssŭ* in Chinese, *harusame* in Japanese) may be substituted for the seaweed vermicelli indicated above. In this case, vermicelli should be dipped briefly into boiling water and drained.

Chopped Spinach Salad

Ingredients:

1 lb. spinach
1/2 cup dried shrimp
2 slices boiled ham, chopped
1 tsp. salt
2 tbsps. sesame oil
1/2 tsp. monosodium gluta-
mate
1/2 cake bean curd
Dressing:
3 tbsps. soy sauce
3 tbsps. salad oil
3 tbsps. vinegar

Method: 1. Soak dried shrimp in hot water for 20 minutes, drain, and chop. 2. Dissolve 1 tsp. salt in boiling water and cook spinach for 3 minutes. 3. Remove from water, drain thoroughly, chop, and sprinkle with sesame oil and monosodium glutamate. 4. Dip bean curd in boiling water, squeeze in cheesecloth to remove water, and break up into small pieces. 5. Place spinach in bottom of a bowl and arrange chopped ham, shrimp, and bean curd on top of it in three equal wedges. 6. Chill in refrigerator before serving. 7. Mix dressing ingredients and serve in separate dish. 8. At table, mix salad ingredients well, add dressing, and serve.

Pork, Spinach, and Tomato Salad

Ingredients:

1/2 lb. tomatoes, peeled and
sliced
1/2 lb. spinach, boiled and
cut into 1 1/4-inch lengths
1/4 lb. shredded pork
1 tbsp. soy sauce
1 tsp. cornstarch
3 tbsps. oil
Sauce:
1 tsp. ginger juice
1 tbsp. sesame oil
1 tbsp. soy sauce
Dash monosodium glutamate

Method: 1. Blanch tomatoes, remove skins, and slice. 2. Boil spinach until tender and cut into 1 1/4-inch lengths. 3. Dredge shredded pork with 1 tbsp. soy sauce and 1 tsp. cornstarch. 4. Heat 3 tbsps. oil and fry pork until color changes. 5. Mix sauce ingredients. 6. Arrange spinach, tomato slices, and fried meat on a plate. 7. Just before serving, cover with sauce mixture. Serve cold.

Vegetables &
Salads

123

Turnip Salad

Ingredients:

1 lb. turnips
1 tsp. salt
2 tbsps. sesame oil
1 tsp. sugar

2 tbsps. soy sauce
2 tbsps. vinegar
1/4 tsp. monosodium glutamate

Method: 1. Shred turnips, sprinkle with salt, soak in water for 1 hour, rinse, and drain. Squeeze off excess water. 2. Mix seasonings in bowl and combine with shredded turnips. Serve cold.

Jellyfish with Turnips

Ingredients:

1 cup shredded jellyfish
2 cups shredded turnips or giant white radish
2 tbsps. chopped onion
1 tsp. salt

1 tbsp. soy sauce
1 tsp. sugar
1 tbsp. vinegar
3 tbsps. sesame oil

Method: 1. Wash jellyfish, place in lukewarm water, and soak overnight. Drain, remove red matter, and shred jellyfish. 2. Shred turnips (or radish), sprinkle with 1 tsp. salt, and let stand for 20 minutes. Squeeze out resulting brine. 3. Mix shredded jellyfish and turnips with onions, soy sauce, sugar, vinegar, and sesame oil. Serve cold.

Jellyfish with Chicken and Cucumber

Ingredients:

2 cups shredded jellyfish
1 cup shredded boiled chicken
4 cups shredded cucumber

Sauce:
2 tbsps. vinegar
3 tbsps. soy sauce
1 tsp. ground mustard
2 tbsps. sesame oil
1/2 tsp. monosodium glutamate

Method: 1. Wash jellyfish in salt water, place in lukewarm water, and soak overnight. Rinse, drain, and shred. (Jellyfish should not be placed in hot water.) 2. Boil chicken until tender, allow to cool, and shred. 3. Wash cucumbers in salt water and shred. 4. Arrange shredded ingredients on a plate. 5. Mix sauce ingredients in a bowl and pour sauce over shredded ingredients before serving.

Note: Jellyfish may be soaked in water for weeks. Change water every day and use jellyfish as needed.

Chinese Pickles

Ingredients:

- 7 cups cabbage, as cut into small pieces
- 6 cups cucumber, as cut into eighths
- 6 cups small turnips, as quartered
- 4 cups carrot, as quartered and cut into 2-inch pieces
- 4 cups celery, as cut into 2-inch pieces
- 6 slices ginger
- 10 whole red peppers
- 30 black peppercorns
- 1/4 lb. salt
- 1 tbsp. wine
- 2 tsps. monosodium glutamate
- 15 cups water (more or less)

Method: 1. Wash vegetable ingredients, cut them as directed above, wipe with cheesecloth, and allow to dry for half a day. 2. Bring 15 cups water to a boil and add all seasonings. Allow to cool. 3. Place vegetables in large glass jar or crock and pour seasoning mixture over them. Vegetables should be covered by liquid. 4. The pickled vegetables may be served one day later in summertime, but should be allowed to stand for 3 or 4 days in other seasons.

Note: Pickled vegetables should be removed from liquid with chopsticks or similar instrument to prevent crushing. As vegetables are used up, more may be added to the brine. In this case, 1 tbsp. salt, 1/2 cup wine, and 1 tbsp. brown sugar should be added to brine at same time.

Crab Meat with Cucumber

Ingredients:

1 cup crab meat, fresh or canned	2 tbsps. soy sauce
3/4 lb. cucumbers	1 tsp. sugar
Dressing:	1 tbsp. sesame oil
2 tbsps. vinegar	Dash monosodium glutamate

Method: 1. Remove bones from crab meat. 2. Wash cucumbers with salt water and shred. 3. Place crab meat and shredded cucumbers on a plate. 4. Mix dressing ingredients, pour over crab meat and cucumbers, mix well, and serve chilled.

Sliced Lotus Root

Ingredients :
>*1 lb. lotus root, peeled and*
>*   sliced*
>*2 1/2 tbsps. vinegar*
>*2 1/2 tbsps. soy sauce*
>*1 1/2 tbsps. sugar*
>*1 tbsp. sesame oil*
>*3 chopped red peppers or a*
>*   few drops tabasco*
>*2 tbsps. oil*

Method : 1. Peel and slice lotus root. Soak slices in water for 10 minutes or more to remove iron. 2. Dip slices in boiling water and remove to cold water again. 3. Heat 2 tbsps. oil and fry red peppers until they turn dark in color. Remove peppers and use oil only. 4. Mix red pepper oil with all other seasonings and add lotus root slices. 5. Allow lotus root to stand for a while in seasoning mixture before serving. Serve cold in seasoning mixture.

Sweet and Sour Chinese Cabbage Rolls

Ingredients :

1 lb. Chinese cabbage	*1/2 tbsp. salt*
2 tbsps. oil	*2 tbsps. vinegar*
2 red peppers, cut into thirds and	*2 tbsps. sugar*
* seeded*	*Dash monosodium glutamate*
1 tbsp. soy sauce	

Method : 1. Separate cabbage into individual leaves. Boil leaves for 10 minutes, drain, and rinse with cold water. 2. Cut each leaf into two parts. 3. Roll cabbage to approximate thickness of a leek (about 3/4 inch in diameter) and cut each roll into 1-inch lengths. 4. Arrange cabbage rolls in a bowl. 5. Heat oil, fry red pepper, and add remaining seasonings. 6. Pour hot seasoning mixture over cabbage rolls and let stand for 30 minutes. 7. Chill and serve cold.

Spiced Soy Beans

Ingredients :
>*3 cups green soy beans,*
>*   unshelled*
>*1 tbsp. salt*
>*1 tsp. black pepper*
>*1 clove aniseed*
>*Water for boiling beans*
>*1 tsp. salt*

Method : 1. Cut off ends of soy beans. 2. Bring to a boil sufficient water to cover soy beans. Add 1 tbsp. salt, 1 tsp. chopped red pepper, and 1 clove aniseed. 3: Add soy beans to boiling water, boil for 15 minutes, drain, and sprinkle with 1 tsp. salt. 4. Serve chilled and discard shells when eating.

PASTRIES AND RICE

Spring Rolls
Meat and Vegetable Buns
Pancake Rolls
Ravioli
Fried Meat Cakes
Roasted Meat Dumplings
Steamed Pork Dumplings
Pork Dumplings in Soup
Chinese Noodles
Noodles in Broth
Noodles with Chicken Broth
Braised Pork Loin with Noodles
Fried Noodles
Fried Noodles with Assorted Meat
Noodles with Tientsin Sauce
Chilled Noodles with Sauce
Lotus Seed and Glutinous Rice Congee
Fried Rice Wrapped in Lotus Leaves
Fried Rice with Assorted Meat
Chinese Bread

Cocktail Party

Served with cocktails or soft drinks,
these dishes put people at ease, spark
good conversation.
  Top: Shrimp Toast (page 58)
  Center: Steamed Pork Dumplings
    (page 137)
  Left: Ravioli (page 134)
  Right: Chilled   Noodles   with
    Sauce (page 142)
  Left center and bottom: Ingredi-
    ents and utensils for making
    dumplings

Spring Rolls

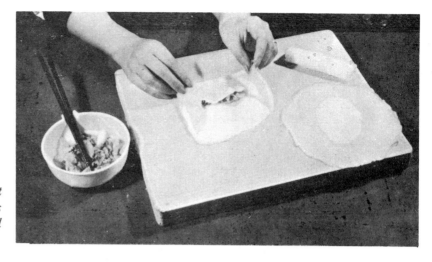

Ingredients for filling:

A

1/2 lb. pork, shredded
1 tbsp. wine
1/2 tsp. salt
1 tsp. cornstarch

10 tbsps. oil

B

1/2 cup shredded leek
2 cups shredded bamboo shoot
1 cup shredded mushrooms
(dried mushrooms, soaked
before shredding)
2 cups bean sprouts
1/4 tsp. salt
2 tbsps. soy sauce

Oil for deep-frying

Method for making filling: 1. Mix A ingredients, sauté with 4 tbsps. oil, and remove to a bowl. 2. Heat 6 tbsps. oil and sauté B ingredients. Mix with sautéed A ingredients and allow to cool.

Ingredients and method for making wrappings: There are three ways to make wrappings for Spring Rolls. These are as follows:

1. Mix 2 cups flour, 2 eggs, and 2 1/2 cups water and stir until smooth. Grease a 7-inch frying pan with a very small amount of oil and heat it. Pour only enough batter into pan to form as thin a "pancake" as possible. As soon as it sets (about 1 minute), remove from pan to a plate. Repeat process until batter is used up.

2. Mix 2 cups flour and 1 cup water to form smooth batter. Using a pastry brush, brush batter in a 5-inch square on a slightly greased and heated pan. When batter sets, remove from pan. Repeat process until batter is used up.

3. Using 2 cups flour and 1 cup water, add water to flour gradually and mix until dough is as soft as marshmallow. Let dough stand overnight. Grease pan very lightly and heat it. Take the mass of dough in your hand and rub it over bottom of pan. A thin sheet of dough will be left to form a wrapping. Remove from pan and repeat process until dough is used up.

Method for making rolls: 1. Place 2 tbsps. of filling on lower half of wrapping. Moisten left and right edges of wrapping with mixture of cornstarch and water. Fold bottom edge up, left and right edges over, and roll. Moisten top edge with cornstarch-and-water mixture and seal. 2. Heat oil and deep-fry rolls until crisp.

Note: Ready-made wrappings can be obtained at some Chinese restaurants or food stores. Filling may be made with chicken or shrimp instead of pork.

Pastries &
Rice

131

Meat and Vegetable Buns

Ingredients :

A

1 lb. ground pork or beef
1 tsp. minced ginger
3 tbsps. chopped onion or leek
6 dried mushrooms, soaked in
    water and chopped
1 lb. spinach or cabbage,
    boiled, drained, and chopped
3 tbsps. sesame oil
3 tbsps. salad oil
4 tbsps. soy sauce
1 tsp. salt
1 tsp. sugar
2 tbsps. wine
1/2 tsp. monosodium
    glutamate

B

8 cups flour
2 tbsps. sugar
1/2 tsp. salt
3 tbsps. oil
8 tsps. dry yeast
4 cups warm water (more or
    less, according to quality
    of flour)

Method :   1. Mix all A ingredients thoroughly in a bowl to form filling for buns.   2. Mix dry yeast with water and add to flour. Add other B ingredients and knead into a soft dough. After dough is well kneaded, place in floured bowl and cover. Allow dough to rise for 3 hours in a warm place. 3. When dough has risen, knead it again on a flour-sprinkled board and roll it into a long sausage. Cut sausage into 1-inch lengths, flatten these pieces, and roll each out to the size of a saucer to form wrapping.   4. Put 1 tbsp. of filling in center of each wrapping, flute edges of wrapping, bring edges together to form a sack, and seal by giving a slight twist and pinching with thumb and forefinger.   5. Place buns in steamer rack on a wet cloth and steam for 15 to 20 minutes.

Note :   Leftover buns may be served after reheating, either by steaming or frying. The filling (A) may also be fried to produce an altogether different and delightful flavor.

Pancake Rolls

Ingredients :
  2 cups flour
  1 cup boiling water (or less)
  2 tbsps. sesame oil
  3 oz. bean paste (mien chiang in Chinese, miso in Japanese)

  1/2 tbsp. soy sauce
  3 tbsps. water
  3 tbsps. oil
  Dash monosodium glutamate

Method : 1. Mix flour with boiling water to form dough mixture. Knead for about 10 minutes into a soft dough. 2. Shape dough into a long sausage and cut into pieces of golf-ball size. Flatten pieces with palm of hand. 3. Brush half of pieces with a little sesame oil and cover each with an unoiled piece. Roll these sandwiches out to pancakes about 5 inches in diameter. 4. Fry pancakes on both sides in flat ungreased pan over low flame. Remove from pan and pull the two halves apart. 5. Steam these pancakes before serving; then fold each into quarters. Yield is about 12 pancakes. Cover with cloth or napkin until ready to serve. 6. Mix remaining ingredients to make bean paste sauce. 7. Pancakes are spread with bean paste sauce and used as wrapping for a little of each of the following dishes, with which they should be served: Scrambled Eggs with Shrimp, Fried Bean Sprouts with Green Peppers, Fried Shredded Potatoes, Sliced White Pork, Fried Pork with Spring Onions. 8. After bean paste sauce and small amounts of above foods have been placed on pancake by individual diner, he rolls it to form a kind of round sandwich and eats it with his fingers. Flavor of pancake rolls is enhanced by spreading chopped onion over bean paste before adding other ingredients.

Pastries &
Rice

133

Ravioli

Ingredients for filling:
1/4 lb. chicken meat, minced or ground
1 tsp. ginger juice
1/2 tsp. salt
1 tbsp. soy sauce
1 tbsp. sesame oil
1 tsp. wine
1 tbsp. chopped celery

Ingredients for sauce:
3 tbsps. sugar
2 tbsps. soy sauce
1 tbsp. wine
1 tbsp. catsup
1 1/2 tbsps. vinegar
1/2 tbsp. cornstarch
1/2 cup water

Ingredients for wrapping:
2 cups flour
1 cup water
1 tsp. salt
1/2 tsp. baking powder mixed with 1 tbsp. water
Cornstarch for rolling dough

Method: 1. Mix all filling ingredients thoroughly in a bowl. 2. Mix flour, water, salt, and baking soda to form dough for wrappings; knead until smooth; and let stand for 30 minutes. 3. Sprinkle breadboard with cornstarch and roll dough very thin. Cut it into 2 1/2-inch squares. 4. Place 1/2 tsp. of filling in center of each square. Fold corners toward center in envelope-style and seal edges with mixture of cornstarch and water. 5. Heat oil and deep-fry ravioli until golden brown. 6. Mix all sauce ingredients except cornstarch and water. Heat sauce and add mixture of cornstarch and water when it comes to a boil. Bring sauce to a boil once again and serve with ravioli as a dip.

Note: Ravioli can be served with sauce as an hors d'œuvre or boiled in soup as a main dish. Ready-made wrappings are available in Japan and China. They are called *hun t'ung pi* in Chinese, *wantan no kawa* in Japanese.

Fried Meat Cakes

Ingredients :

1/2 lb. finely ground pork	*1 tbsp. wine*
1/4 lb. round or Chinese cabbage	*6 tbsps. oil*
1 stalk leek, chopped	*2 eggs, beaten with 1/2 tsp. salt*
1 tsp. minced ginger	*3 cups flour*
3 tbsps. soy sauce	*1 1/2 cups boiling water (vary*
1/2 tsp. salt	*according to quality of flour)*
1/2 tsp. monosodium glutamate	*Oil for deep-frying*

Method : 1. Heat 3 tbsps. oil in frying pan and fry leek, ginger, and ground pork. Add soy sauce, salt, monosodium glutamate, and wine. Remove to a bowl. 2. Heat 3 more tbsps. oil and fry beaten eggs. Break eggs into small pieces and add to meat mixture. 3. Wash cabbage and chop it fine. Sprinkle with salt and squeeze out water. 4. Add cabbage to meat and egg mixture and mix thoroughly to make filling for meat cakes. 5. Mix flour with boiling water and knead into a soft dough. Cover with damp cloth and allow to stand for 10 minutes before using. 6. Roll dough on board into a long sausage and cut into pieces about the size of a golf ball. 7. Sprinkle board with flour and roll each ball into a thin "pancake." 8. Place 2 tbsps. filling mixture between 2 pancakes and pinch edges together. 9. Heat deep oil and fry meat cakes until light brown. Serve with soy sauce and vinegar.

Roasted Meat Dumplings

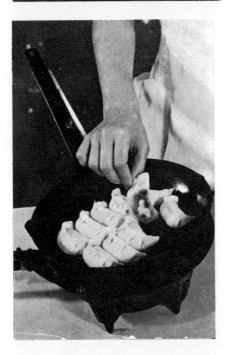

Ingredients :

A

1/2 lb. ground beef or pork
1/2 medium onion, finely chopped
1 tbsp. sesame oil
1/2 tsp. salt
2 tbsps. soy sauce
1 tsp. minced ginger
1 tbsp. wine
4 tbsps. oil
3 tbsps. water

B

2 cups flour
1 cup boiling water (more or less, according to quality of flour)
2 tbsps. oil
2 cups water

Method : 1. Place all A ingredients in bowl and mix thoroughly to make filling. 2. Mix flour and boiling water to form dough for wrapping. Cover dough with damp cloth and let stand for 30 minutes. 3. Knead dough well and form into a long sausage. Cut into 1-inch lengths. 4. Sprinkle board with flour, flatten pieces of dough with palm of hand, and roll out very thin to form doilies about 3 inches in diameter. 5. Place about 1 tsp. of filling in center of each doily. Fold over in half-moon shape and pinch edges together. Yield will be about 40 dumplings. 6. Using 1/2 tbsp. oil per 10 dumplings, heat oil in frying pan, arrange dumplings pressed together in rows, and fry until bottom turns brown. If small pan is used, process can be repeated until all dumplings have been fried. 7. Using 1/2 cup of water per 10 dumplings, pour water over fried dumplings, cover with lid, and cook until water is absorbed.   8. Serve hot, browned side up, allowing dumplings to remain stuck together in rows.

Note : Do not let dry flour stick to edges of rolled-out doilies, since this will prevent sealing when edges are pinched together. In making dough, vary amount of water according to relative dryness or moisture of flour.

Steamed Pork Dumplings

Ingredients :

A

1/2 lb. ground pork
1/2 lb. small boiled shrimp, shelled and chopped
2 tbsps. sesame oil
2 tbsps. salad oil or lard
3 tbsps. water
3 tbsps. soy sauce
1/2 tsp. salt
2 tsps. wine

1 tsp. chopped ginger
1/4 lb. celery or spring onion, chopped

B

3 cups flour
1 1/2 cups boiling water

Method :   1. Mix all A ingredients thoroughly in a bowl to form filling for dumplings.   2. Mix flour with boiling water (B ingredients) until it forms a soft dough.   3. Knead dough until smooth, cover with damp cheese-cloth, and let stand for 1/2 hour before rolling out.   4. Sprinkle dry flour on board and roll dough into a sausage about 1 inch in diameter. Cut sausage into 1-inch pieces.   5. Flatten these pieces and roll each into a round doily about 3 inches in diameter. Center of doily must be thicker than edges.   6. To make dumplings, place 1 tsp. of filling in center of each doily, fold over to form half-moon shape, and pinch edges together. (Recipe makes about 50 dumplings.)   7. When all dumplings have been made, place them on a damp cloth on a steamer rack (or in a double boiler) and steam for 15 minutes. Do not pile dumplings on top of one another for steaming. Either use two-level steamer or repeat steaming process until all dumplings have been steamed.

Pork Dumplings in Soup

Ingredients :

A

1/2 lb. ground pork
3 tbsps. water
2 tbsps. salad oil or lard
2 tbsps. sesame oil
3 tbsps. soy sauce
1/2 tsp. salt
2 tsps. wine
3 tbsps. chopped onion

1 tsp. chopped ginger
1/2 lb. Chinese cabbage, chopped
   fine

B

3 cups flour
1 1/2 cups water

Method : 1. Wash Chinese cabbage, chop it fine, sprinkle with salt, and squeeze out water with cheesecloth. 2. Mix all A ingredients (including cabbage) thoroughly in a bowl. 3. Mix flour with cold water to form a soft dough. 4. Knead dough until smooth, cover with damp cheesecloth, and let stand 1/2 hour before rolling out. 5. Sprinkle board with dry flour and roll dough into sausage about 1 inch in diameter. Cut into 1-inch pieces. 6. Flatten these pieces and roll each into a round doily about 2 1/2 inches in diameter. Center of doily must be thicker than edges. 7. To make dumplings, place 1 tsp. of filling (mixture A) in center of each doily, fold over to form half-moon shape, and pinch edges together. (Recipe makes about 50 dumplings.) 8. Drop dumplings one by one into boiling water. When water boils up again, add 1 cup cold water. Repeat this process two more times. 9. Dip dumplings out into dishes for individual servings, allowing some of boiling water to cover them like a soup. Serve hot dumplings with separate dishes of soy sauce and vinegar for dipping.

Chinese Noodles

Ingredients :
   4 eggs

3 cups flour (or more)

Method : 1. Beat eggs lightly, mix with flour, and knead into soft dough. 2. Cover dough with damp cloth and allow to stand for 20 minutes. 3. Knead again. Sprinkle flour on board and roll dough very thin. 4. Fold dough into 4 or 5 pleats or layers. Cut across the pleats as finely as possible, in order to make long, thin strands (see photos on facing page).

Since most Chinese noodles are made without eggs, the following recipe may be substituted for the one above:

Ingredients :
   3 cups hard flour
   1 1/2 cups water

Dash salt

Method : Same as for recipe above.

Note : The recipes above will make enough noodles for three persons. Ready-made noodles, fresh or dried, can be obtained at Chinese groceries.

Noodles in Broth

Ingredients :

1/2 lb. pork, shredded
1 stalk leek, shredded
1/2 lb. spinach, washed and cut
   into 3 sections
10 cups water
4 tbsps. soy sauce

1 tsp. salt
1/4 tsp. monosodium glutamate
5 tbsps. oil
1/2 lb. Chinese noodles, cooked
1 egg, beaten

Method : 1. Heat 5 tbsps. oil in pan sufficiently deep for broth. Fry pork, leek, and spinach. 2. Add water and seasonings and bring to a boil. 3. Add previously cooked noodles (see recipe for Noodles with Tientsin Sauce, page 142), and when broth boils up again, add beaten egg slowly, stirring lightly at same time. Serve hot.

Pastries &
Rice

139

Noodles with Chicken Broth

Ingredients :

1/4 lb. noodles, cooked

1/4 cup shredded cooked chicken

1/4 cup shredded cooked ham

1/4 cup shredded cooked pork

1 1/2 cups broth from cooked chicken

1/3 tsp. salt

Dash pepper

1/6 tsp. monosodium glutamate

Method : 1. Place cooked noodles in serving bowl. 2. Arrange chicken, ham, and pork on top of noodles. 3. Heat broth from cooked chicken, adding seasonings. 4. Pour hot broth over noodles and serve hot.

Braised Pork Loin with Noodles

Ingredients :

1/2 lb. pork loin

1 tbsp. soy sauce

1 tbsp. wine

1 tbsp. chopped leek

1/2 tsp. chopped ginger

1 tsp. black pepper

1 tbsp. oil

1 tsp. sugar

2 cups broth

1 tsp. salt

1 tbsp. soy sauce

1 tsp. wine

5 small bowls cooked noodles (individual servings)

Method : 1. Soak pork loin for 20 minutes in mixture of soy sauce, wine, leek, ginger, and black pepper. Save the liquid. 2. Heat 1 tbsp. oil and fry pork on both sides until color turns to light brown. 3. Add sugar and liquid from soaking. Boil until liquid evaporates. 4. Remove pork from pan and cut into small pieces. 5. Heat broth, adding salt, soy sauce, and wine. Bring to a boil. 6. Place boiled noodles in bowl or casserole, pour in hot broth, and place pork on top. Serve hot.

Fried Noodles

Ingredients :

1/2 lb. Chinese noodles

5 eggs, beaten with 1/2 tsp. salt

2 bamboo shoots, shredded

1/2 lb. pork, shredded

1 lb. spinach, cut into 3 sections

6 dried mushrooms, soaked in water and shredded

1 stalk leek, shredded

1 tbsp. wine

2 tbsps. soy sauce

2 tsps. salt

1/4 tsp. monosodium glutamate

11 tbsps. oil

Method : 1. Boil noodles until tender, drain, rinse with cold water, and drain again. 2. Beat eggs, adding 1/2 tsp. salt, and fry in 3 tbsps. oil.

Break fried egg into small pieces and remove to a plate. 3. Heat 3 tbsps. oil and fry bamboo shoot, pork, spinach, mushrooms, and leek, adding wine, soy sauce, and monosodium glutamate. Remove to a plate. 4. Heat 5 tbsps. oil. Fry noodles for 6 minutes, stirring constantly and adding 2 tsps. salt. 5. Remove noodles to a large plate or bowl, cover with other fried ingredients, and serve hot.

Fried Noodles with Assorted Meat

Ingredients :

5 small bowls cooked noodles (individual servings)

1/4 lb. sliced pork, dredged with 1 tsp. soy sauce and 1 tsp. cornstarch

1/4 lb. sliced chicken, dredged with 1/2 tsp. salt and 1/2 tsp. cornstarch

2 abalone, sliced

5 dried mushrooms, soaked and sliced

1/4 lb. bamboo shoot, sliced

25 shrimps (or 4 sliced prawns), dredged with 1 tsp. wine and 1 tsp. cornstarch

40 snow peas, strung and parboiled

1/4 lb. ham, sliced

7 tbsps. oil

4 cups water or broth

2 tbsps. wine

2 tbsps. soy sauce

1 tsp. salt

Method : 1. Heat 3 tbsps. oil and fry noodles in one big pancake until both sides turn light brown. Remove to a plate. 2. Heat 4 tbsps. oil and fry pork, chicken, abalone, mushrooms, bamboo shoot, shrimp, snow peas, and ham. 3. Add water (or broth) and seasonings. Bring to boil and thicken with cornstarch. 4. Pour mixture over fried noodles and serve hot.

Note : This recipe serves 4 to 6 persons.

Noodles with Tientsin Sauce

Ingredients:

    1 lb. ground pork
    1 lb. soy bean paste (mien chiang in Chinese, miso in Japanese)
    4 tbsps. soy sauce
    1 cup water
    2 stalks leek, chopped
    1 tsp. minced ginger
    5 tbsps. oil
    2 tbsps. sugar
    1/2 lb. Chinese noodles

Method: 1. Mix bean paste, soy sauce, and water thoroughly. 2. Heat 5 tbsps. oil and fry pork, leek, and ginger. When meat changes color, add bean paste mixture. 3. Simmer for 15 minutes, add sugar, and serve hot in separate dish. 4. Drop noodles into boiling water. When water boils up again, add 1 cup cold water. Repeat this process two more times. When noodles are tender, drain and serve in individual bowls. Bean paste is dipped over noodles before they are eaten.

Note: Several or all of the following cold dishes will go well with this noodle dish: 5 cucumbers, soaked in salt water and shredded; 5 green peppers, seeded and shredded; 1/2 lb. bean sprouts (heads and tails removed), dipped in boiling water for 2 minutes and rinsed in cold water; 5 eggs, beaten, fried in a thin layer, and shredded.

Chilled Noodles with Sauce

Ingredients:

    3/4 lb. Chinese noodles
    1 tbsp. sesame oil
    2 eggs
    1 cup cooked shredded beef or pork
    1/2 cup shredded boiled ham
    1 cup shredded cucumber
    1/2 cup cooked shelled shrimp

Sauce:

    2 tbsps. sesame oil
    1/2 tsp. salt
    1 tbsp. sesame paste
    1 tbsp. red pepper oil or 1 tsp. tabasco
    2 tbsps. soy sauce
    2 tsps. vinegar
    2 cups broth or water
    1/4 tsp. monosodium glutamate

Method: 1. Drop noodles into boiling water. When water boils up again, add cold water and bring to boil once more. Drain noodles, mix with 1 tbsp. sesame oil, and chill in refrigerator. 3. Beat eggs and fry in thin layers with small amount of oil. Shred fried egg. 4. Arrange shredded eggs, beef, ham, cucumber, and shrimp on top of chilled noodles. 5. Make sesame paste by grinding sesame seeds in mortar. 6. Make red pepper oil by heating 2 tbsps. oil and frying 3 red peppers until they turn dark. Remove peppers and use oil only. 7. Mix all sauce ingredients thoroughly and serve sauce separately in a bowl. Pour sauce over noodles and shredded ingredients just before eating.

Note : Peanut butter may be substituted for sesame paste.

Lotus Seed and Glutinous Rice Congee

Ingredients :

1 cup glutinous rice	3 oz. sugar
1/2 cup dried lotus seeds	

Method : 1. Soak lotus seeds in hot water and remove thick skin. Push out bitter green hearts with a toothpick. Wash seeds and boil in 3 pints (9 cups) of water over low flame for 30 minutes. 2. Wash rice and add to lotus seeds. Boil until rice becomes soft. 3. Add sugar and mix well. Serve hot.

Fried Rice Wrapped in Lotus Leaves

Ingredients :

3 cups boiled rice	1 tbsp. soy sauce
8 small dried mushrooms, soaked and diced	1/2 tsp. sugar
	1/2 tsp. salt
1 cup diced barbecue pork	Dash pepper
1 cup small shrimp, boiled in salt water and shelled	2 tbsps. sesame oil
	3 to 6 lotus leaves, parboiled

Method : 1. Heat oil and sauté mushrooms, pork, and shrimp. Add rice and stir well. 2. Add seasonings, stirring constantly. Remove mixture from heat. 3. Spread lotus leaves and place portion of rice mixture in middle of each. Wrap rice in envelope style and tie with stem of lotus leaf. 4. Steam leaf-wrapped rice for 10 minutes, allowing it to absorb flavor of leaf. Before serving, slit each leaf with sharp knife. Serve hot and discard lotus leaves when eating.

Note : Either fresh or dried lotus leaves may be used.

Fried Rice with Assorted Meat

Ingredients:

8 small bowls cooked rice, cold
1 leek, finely chopped
3 eggs, beaten with a dash of salt
1/4 lb. chicken meat, cooked
1/4 lb. bamboo shoot
1/4 lb. shrimp, shelled, cleaned,
    and boiled

1/4 lb. ham
6 dried mushrooms, soaked and
    chopped
1/4 lb. green peas, cooked
9 tbsps. oil

Method: 1. Cut cooked chicken meat, bamboo shoot, ham, and mushrooms into 1/2-inch squares. 2. Heat 4 tbsps. oil, fry beaten eggs, break into small pieces, and remove to a plate. 3. Heat remaining 5 tbsps. oil and fry leek, chicken, bamboo shoot, shrimp, ham, mushrooms, and peas. 4. Add rice and stir constantly over low flame. Salt to taste. 5. Add fried eggs and mix thoroughly. Serve hot.

Note: This recipe serves 8 persons.

Chinese Bread

Ingredients:

A

10 cups flour
10 tsps. dry yeast
2 tbsps. sugar
1 tsp. salt
5 cups lukewarm water
    (quantity to be decided
    according to moisture
    of flour)

B

3 tbsps. sesame oil
3 tbsps. chopped onion
1 tsp. salt
1/2 tsp. pepper

Method: 1. Mix all A ingredients to form a smooth dough. 2. Place dough in a bowl and let rise for 3 hours over hot water (not too hot). Never touch dough while it is rising. 3. After dough has risen, roll it out thin and sprinkle lightly with B ingredients. 4. Roll dough like a jelly roll. Cut into 2-inch lengths. Using a chopstick or similar implement, press down on center of each piece and pinch upper edges together to form an open-ended bun. 5. Steam buns for 15 minutes before serving.

CASSEROLES AND SOUPS

Fire Kettle
Assorted Meat in Casserole
Chicken and Spinach Soup
Velvet Chicken and Sweet Corn Soup
Whole Chicken Soup
Egg Flower Soup with Cucumbers
Melon Soup
Tomato Soup with Egg Flower
Beef Soup with Quail Eggs
Tomato and Meat Cake Soup
Shredded Meat and Vegetable Soup
Egg Roll Soup
Birds' Nest Soup with Flowing Egg White
Birds' Nest Soup with Chicken
Meat Ball Soup with Chinese Cabbage
Lotus Root and Pork Soup
Chinese Cabbage Soup with Shrimp Omelets
Meat and Shrimp Ball Soup
Abalone Soup with Meat Balls
Shark's Fin Soup

HAPPY DINNER TIME

These are the dishes best liked by the people of East and West. The quantity depends upon the number of guests, and the quality upon the family's economic condition. Amount shown is enough for six— either family or company. After preparation, it takes only 15 minutes to cook these dishes. The secret will be found on page 18.

Fire Kettle

Ingredients:

3 tbsps. chopped leek

2 tbsps. grated ginger

1/2 cup shrimp, shelled and cleaned (or dried shrimp, soaked and drained)

1/2 cup dried scallops, soaked and drained

1/2 head Chinese cabbage, chopped

1 bamboo shoot, sliced thin

1/2 lb. pork, sliced thin

1/2 lb. beef, sliced thin

1/2 lb. boned chicken, sliced

1/2 lb. fresh oysters, washed in salt water

6 dried mushrooms, soaked in lukewarm water and halved

1/2 lb. small-size fish, boned

1 oz. vermicelli, dipped in boiling water and drained

1 tsp. salt

3 tbsps. wine

10 cups broth or water

Method: In northern China, where the winters are bitterly cold, this dish is cooked in a fire kettle: a large vessel with a central chimney into which glowing charcoal is placed to cook the ingredients. The fire kettle stands on legs and has a lid with a central hole to accommodate the chimney. A satisfactory substitute for the fire kettle is a Dutch oven (with lid) placed upon a charcoal brazier like a Japanese *hibachi*. 1. Prepare all meat, sea food, and vegetable ingredients as directed above. 2. Before placing Dutch oven on brazier (or charcoal in fire kettle), arrange ingredients in it as follows: chopped leek, ginger, shrimp, and scallops on the bottom; Chinese cabbage next; and on top of this the sliced meat ingredients, bamboo shoot, mushrooms, oysters, fish, and vermicelli. 3. Sprinkle 1 tsp. salt and 3 tbsps. wine over ingredients, add broth, and place Dutch oven on fire. Cover and allow to cook until ingredients become tender. If genuine fire kettle is used, put lid on first; then place glowing charcoal inside chimney. 4. Dish should cook at table, so that diners may help themselves from it when ingredients are sufficiently cooked. Food is eaten from small individual bowls (rice bowls) along with soup in which it has cooked.

Note: Any of ingredients may be omitted or replaced by others. Ingredients should not be stirred during cooking, so that diners may help themselves to those they prefer. If desired, Dutch oven may be placed on brazier first, provided small amount of water or broth is poured in before other ingredients are added.

Assorted Meat in Casserole

Ingredients :

3 oz. chicken meat

3 oz. pork

3 oz. ham

2 oz. bamboo shoot

4 dried mushrooms, soaked and stemmed

3 oz. shrimp, shelled and cleaned

5 dried scallops, soaked in boiling water for 20 minutes

1 cup chopped green vegetables

4 cups water

2 tsps. salt

1 tbsp. wine

Method : Dice chicken, pork, ham, bamboo shoot, and mushrooms. 2. Heat 4 cups water, add all other ingredients, and cover with lid. 3. Boil for 15 minutes and serve hot in casserole dish.

Note : Any one of ingredients may be omitted if unobtainable.

Chicken and Spinach Soup

Ingredients :

1/2 lb. chicken

1 onion, sliced

3 slices ginger

1/2 lb. spinach

1 oz. vermicelli

1 tbsp. salt

1 tbsp. wine

1/4 tsp. monosodium glutamate

Method : 1. Boil chicken with onion and ginger in ample water for 1 hour or until tender. Remove chicken to a plate and save broth for soup. 2. Wash spinach and cut into sections. 3. Soak vermicelli in hot water and cut into sections. 4. Bring soup to boil, add spinach, vermicelli, and seasonings. Cook until spinach is tender. 5. Shred chicken and add to soup. Serve hot.

Velvet Chicken with Sweet Corn Soup

Ingredients :

1/4 lb. minced chicken fillet

1 tsp. wine

1 tsp. salt

2 egg whites, lightly beaten

10 cups chicken broth, with 1 tbsp. salt added

1 can cream-style sweet corn

1/2 tsp. monosodium glutamate

Method : 1. Mince chicken fillet and mix well with wine, salt, and beaten egg whites. 2. Bring chicken broth to boil, add sweet corn and chicken mixture, and bring to boil again. 3. Add monosodium glutamate and serve hot.

Whole Chicken Soup

Ingredients:

1 spring chicken	1 lb. cut vegetables
1 stalk leek	2 tbsps. wine
10 quail eggs	2 tsps. salt (Vary according to taste.)

Method: 1. Boil chicken with leek and sufficient water for 40 minutes or until tender. 2. Boil quail eggs and soak in water; shell. 3. Add vegetables, quail eggs, and seasonings and simmer for 20 minutes. Serve hot. 4. Tear chicken apart before dish is served. Serve small dishes of soy sauce for dipping chicken.

Egg Flower Soup with Cucumbers

Ingredients:

1/2 lb. pork, sliced	2 cucumbers, sliced
2 tsps. wine	12 cups broth or water
2 tsps. soy sauce	2 eggs, lightly beaten
2 tsps. cornstarch	Salt to taste
4 tbsps. oil	Dash monosodium glutamate
1/2 stalk leek, cut into small pieces	

Method: 1. Dredge pork slices with wine, soy sauce, and cornstarch. 2. Heat oil in deep pan and fry pork with leek. 3. When pork turns brown, add broth. 4. After soup comes to a boil, add cucumber slices, salt, and monosodium glutamate. 5. Slowly stir in beaten egg.

Note: Chicken or beef may be substituted for pork.

Melon Soup

Ingredients :

 1 *white gourd melon (tung kua in Chinese, tōgan in Japanese), about 4 lbs.*
 1/4 *lb. chicken fillet, diced*
 1/4 *lb. ham, diced*
 3 *dried mushrooms, soaked and diced*
 1 *small bamboo shoot, diced*
 1/4 *lb. shrimp, shelled and cleaned*
 6 *cups chicken stock*
 1 *tbsp. salt*
 1 *stalk leek, cut into small sections*
 2 *slices ginger*
 1 *tsp. wine*

Method : 1. Cut off top of melon about 1/4 of the way down. Scoop out seeds and spongy material. Notch edge for more attractive effect. Parboil melon for 15 minutes and remove to a plate. 2. Combine all other ingredients and steam melon with these for 1 hour, or boil melon in mixture for 30 minutes. 3. Remove melon to serving dish, fill with soup, and pour remaining soup around it.

Tomato Soup with Egg Flower

Ingredients :

 2 *medium-size tomatoes (about 1 lb.)*
 1 *medium-size round onion (about 1/2 lb.)*
 3 *tbsps. lard*
 6 *cups broth*
 1 *tbsp. wine*
 2 *tsps. salt*
 Dash *pepper*
 1/4 *tsp. monosodium glutamate*
 1 *egg*

Method : Peel onion and cut into 8 crescent-shaped sections. 2. Blanch tomatoes, remove skin, and cut into 8 crescent-shaped sections. 3. Heat 3 tbsps. lard, sauté onion and tomato, and add broth and seasonings. 4. Beat egg. After soup boils up, add egg slowly, stirring at the same time. Serve hot.

Beef Soup with Quail Eggs

Ingredients :

 1/2 *lb. beef, sliced*
 10 *quail eggs*
 10 *snow peas*
 6 *cups water*
 2 *tsps. salt*
 1/2 *tsp. monosodium glutamate*

Method : 1. Hard-boil quail eggs and remove shells. 2. Heat water and add sliced beef when water boils. Skim off froth. 3. When beef is tender, add salt, monosodium glutamate, eggs, and snow peas. Serve hot.

Tomato and Meat Cake Soup

Ingredients :
1/4 lb. ground beef or pork
1 egg
1/2 tsp. salt
1 tbsp. bread crumbs
10 small dried mushrooms, soaked and stemmed (Save juice.)
2 tomatoes, skinned and quartered
1/2 lb. spinach, cut into 2-inch sections
7 cups broth
1 tbsp. salt

Method : 1. Mix ground meat with egg, 1/2 tsp. salt, bread crumbs, and 2 tbsps. juice from soaked mushrooms. Form into 10 patties. 2. Squeeze water from soaked mushrooms and place one meat patty on top of each. 3. Steam patties for 10 minutes. 4. Heat broth and add tomatoes and steamed meat cakes. Bring to boil and add spinach and 1 tbsp. salt. Bring to boil again and serve hot.

Shredded Meat and Vegetable Soup

Ingredients :
4 cups shredded cabbage
1/4 cup shredded uncooked chicken fillet (2 oz.)
1/2 tsp. wine
1/2 tsp. ginger juice
1/4 cup shredded ham (2 oz.)
1/4 cup shredded bamboo shoot (2 oz.)
5 dried mushrooms, soaked in hot water for 15 minutes and shredded

1/2 tsp. salt
1 tsp. cornstarch
A little lard
Soup:
10 cups chicken broth
1 tbsp. wine
1 tbsp. salt
1/2 tsp. monosodium glutamate

Method : 1. Boil shredded cabbage and drain thoroughly. 2. Shred chicken fillet and mix with 1/2 tsp. wine and 1/2 tsp. ginger juice. 3. Sprinkle chicken, ham, cabbage, bamboo shoot, and mushrooms with 1/2 tsp. salt and 1 tsp. cornstarch. 4. Rub inside of a bowl with a little lard and place chicken, ham, bamboo shoot, and mushrooms in 4 sections of bowl. Cover with shredded cabbage and steam for 15 minutes. 5. Heat chicken broth and add seasonings. 6. Turn out steamed ingredients into a deep bowl and pour in hot soup slowly from edge, so as not to disturb mound of steamed ingredients. Serve hot, breaking mound of ingredients with chopsticks so that diners may easily take some of each.

Casseroles &
Soups

Egg Roll Soup

Ingredients :

A
1/2 lb. ground beef or pork
1 tbsp. wine
1 tsp. cornstarch
1/2 tsp. salt

B
2 eggs
Dash salt
1 tbsp. oil
1/4 lb. carrot, sliced thin
1/4 lb. spinach, cut into 4
  sections
3 tbsps. oil
3 tbsps. soy sauce
2 tbsps. cornstarch, mixed
  with 2 tbsps. water
2 cups broth or water

Method : 1. Mix all A ingredients thoroughly and divide mixture into 4 parts. 2. Beat eggs, adding dash salt. Heat 1 tbsp. oil and fry 4 thin egg sheets. 3. Place meat mixture on egg sheets and form rolls. Use small amount of cornstarch and water to make paste for sealing rolls. 4. Place egg rolls and carrots on plate and steam for 10 minutes. 5. Cut egg rolls on bias into 1/2-inch lengths. 6. Heat 3 tbsps. oil, sauté spinach, and add 2 cups broth or water. When soup boils up, add egg rolls, carrots, soy sauce, and cornstarch mixture. Stir well and serve hot.

Birds' Nest Soup with Flowing Egg White

Ingredients :

4 birds' nests
2 egg whites, beaten
1/4 lb. chicken fillet,
  chopped
1 slice ham, chopped
1 tbsp. parsley, chopped
5 cups chicken broth
2 tsps. salt
1 tbsp. wine
2 tbsps. cornstarch, mixed
  with 6 tbsps. water

Method : 1. Soak birds' nests overnight. Change water and remove feathers with tweezers. 2. Chop chicken fillet, adding a little water after chopping. 3. Chop ham and parsley. 4. Heat broth. Add wine, salt, and chopped chicken and boil for 5 minutes. 5. Add birds' nests and cornstarch mixture and simmer for 10 minutes. 6. Add beaten egg white and serve in a deep dish. Garnish with ham and parsley on top of egg white.

Birds' Nest Soup with Chicken

Ingredients :
4 birds' nests
4 oz. cooked chicken, shredded
4 slices boiled ham, shredded
6 cups chicken soup
1 tbsp. salt
1/2 tsp. monosodium glutamate
4 snow peas, shredded

Method :   1. Soak birds' nests overnight. Change water and remove feathers with tweezers.   2. Heat chicken soup, add salt, and simmer birds' nests in soup for 20 minutes.   3. Add chicken, ham, snow peas, and monosodium glutamate. Serve hot.

Note :   Edible birds' nests are about the size of a soup spoon and are mixed with feathers. They are built by swallows that live on the coasts of the China Sea. The nests, made chiefly from the dried, glutinous saliva of the swallows, are used in making soup. Since the swallows feed upon small fish, the nests have a high protein content. The price of birds' nests will vary, since there are many varieties. The best ones, which have fewer feathers, are imported from the Philippines and North Borneo. Connoisseurs of Chinese cooking consider birds' nest soup one of the tastiest and most expensive of dishes.

Meat Ball Soup with Chinese Cabbage

Ingredients :
1 lb. Chinese cabbage
2 oz. vermicelli
1/2 lb. ground meat
3 tbsps. chopped leek
1 egg
1 tsp. ginger juice
1 tsp. wine
2 1/2 tsps. salt
6 cups broth or water

Method :   1. Cut Chinese cabbage into 2-inch chunks and wash.   2. Soak vermicelli in warm water and drain.   3. Mix ground meat with leek, egg, ginger juice, wine, and 1/2 tsp. salt. Form small meat balls about size of teaspoon.   4. Heat broth, add Chinese cabbage, and boil for 10 minutes. Then add meat balls and boil for 15 minutes. Skim off froth.   5. Add vermicelli and 2 tsps. salt. Serve hot.

Lotus Root and Pork Soup

Ingredients :
1 lb. lotus root
1 1/2 lbs. spareribs
6 cups broth (from spareribs)
1 stalk leek, cut into small sections
2 tsps. salt
1/4 tsp. monosodium glutamate

Method :   1. Discard ends of lotus root. Remove skin and cut root in half lengthwise. Then slice thin. Soak in water with a small amount of vinegar to prevent discoloration.   2. Simmer spareribs for 40 minutes or until tender, using enough water to produce 6 cups broth.   3. Add lotus root, leek, salt, and monosodium glutamate. Simmer for 20 minutes longer and serve hot.

Casseroles &
Soups

155

Chinese Cabbage Soup with Shrimp Omelets

Ingredients :

A

1/2 lb. shrimp
1 tsp. ginger juice
1/2 tsp. salt
1/2 tsp. wine
1/2 tsp. cornstarch

B

3 eggs, beaten
1/2 tsp. salt

C

Soup:
3/4 lb. raw pork bacon or pork loin
1 lb. Chinese cabbage, cut into small pieces
1 oz. bean vermicelli (fên ssŭ in Chinese, harusame in Japanese)
2 tsps. salt
1 tbsp. wine
Dash monosodium glutamate

Method : 1. Shell and clean shrimp. Chop shrimp into fine pieces and mix with other A ingredients. 2. Beat eggs well, adding salt. 3. Heat small amount of oil in ladle or very small frying pan. When ladle is hot, pour in 1 tbsp. beaten egg. Allow egg to set slightly. Then place small quantity of shrimp mixture on egg, fold over, and fry. 4. Repeat this process until all of egg is used. Yield is about 28 small omelets. 5. Boil pork bacon in water for 40 minutes. (If sliced pork loin is used instead of bacon, cooking time is less.) Allow pork to cool and then slice it. Save broth for soup. 6. Cut Chinese cabbage into small pieces. 7. Soak vermicelli in hot water, remove from water, and cut into sections. 8. Heat broth and add sufficient water to make 10 cups. Add pork, cabbage, vermicelli, seasonings, and omelets. Boil for about 30 minutes until cabbage is tender. Serve hot.

Mrs. Ma's
Cookbook

156

Meat and Shrimp Ball Soup

Ingredients:

A

1/2 lb. shrimp, shelled, cleaned, and chopped
1 tsp. cornstarch
2 tsps. wine
1/2 egg white and the yolk
1/2 tsp. salt
1/2 tsp. ginger juice

B

1/2 lb. ground pork
1/2 tsp. salt
1 tsp. wine
1/2 egg white and the yolk
1 tbsp. chopped leek
1/2 tbsp. cornstarch
1 tbsp. soy sauce

C

1/2 lb. spinach, washed and cut into 2 or 3 sections
2/3 lb. bamboo shoot, cut into small, thin slices
6 dried mushrooms, soaked and cut in half
1 oz. vermicelli, cut in half
1 lb. Chinese cabbage, cut into small pieces
8 cups broth
Salt and monosodium glutamate to taste

Method: 1. Mixed chopped shrimp with other A ingredients and shape into small balls with a teaspoon. 2. Mix ground pork thoroughly with B ingredients and shape into small balls of same size as shrimp balls. 3. Heat broth, add all other C ingredients, add shrimp and meat balls, and simmer until ingredients are tender. Serve hot in casserole dish or bowl.

Note: This dish may be cooked in advance and reheated to serve.

Casseroles &
Soups

157

Abalone Soup with Meat Balls

Ingredients:

A	B
1/2 lb. ground beef	1 packet vermicelli (50 grams or
2 tbsps. chopped leek	2 oz.), previously soaked in
1 tsp. minced ginger	warm water
1/2 tsp. salt	4 stalks leek, cut into small pieces
1 tbsp. cornstarch	4 slices ginger
1 tbsp. soy sauce	8 cups broth or water
1 egg	4 canned abalone, sliced
	1/4 lb. Chinese cabbage, cut into
	small sections
	2 tbsps. wine
	2 tsps. salt

Method: 1. Mix A ingredients thoroughly and form into small meat balls about the size of a quarter in diameter. 2. Heat broth and add meat balls and other B ingredients, except wine and salt. 3. When broth boils, add these. Cook until ingredients become tender, and serve hot.

Shark's Fin Soup

Ingredients:

1/4 lb. refined shark's fins	2 tbsps. wine
1/2 chicken	1 tbsp. salt
2 stalks leek	1/2 tsp. monosodium glutamate
10 slices ginger	Sufficient water to make 10 cups
1/2 cup shredded bamboo shoot	chicken broth

Method: 1. Soak shark's fins overnight, rinse in cold water three times, and boil for 1 hour in plenty of water with 1 stalk leek and 5 slices ginger. Rinse and drain. 2. Boil chicken for 1 1/2 hours with 1 stalk leek and 5 slices ginger. Use sufficient water to provide 10 cups broth after boiling. 3. Remove chicken from broth, bone, and shred. 4. Boil shark's fins again in chicken broth for 30 minutes. Then add 1 cup shredded chicken and 1/2 cup shredded bamboo shoot. 5. Add seasonings and serve hot.

DESSERTS

Eight Treasures Rice Pudding
Honeyed Apples
Fried Custard
Fried Sweet Potato Balls
Glazed Sweet Potatoes
Almond Jelly with Mixed Fruit
Fried Cookies
Almond Cookies
Walnut Tea
Full Moon Dumplings

DESSERT

Enjoy this dessert with your friends at tea time or serve its as the climax to a dinner. The picture shows Eight Treasures Rice Pudding, which is made of glutinous rice, dried red and green plums, candied lotus seeds, honey dates, and chestnuts. Each of these fruits has its own distinctive color and flavor. In making the pudding, canned fruit cocktail may be substituted.

Eight Treasures Rice Pudding

Ingredients :

A

2 cups glutinous rice
2 cups cold water
5 tbsps. sugar
1/2 lb. sweet bean paste (or
  1/2 lb. red date paste—
  see "Note" below)
4 tbsps. lard

B

Dried fruits and nuts:
2 oz. dried red and green plums
  (or other candied fruit)
2 oz. candied lotus seeds (or
  blanched almonds)
2 oz. honey dates
2 oz. chestnuts, boiled, shel-
  led, and halved
2 oz. raisins

Sauce:
2 tbsps. sugar
1 tbsp. cornstarch
1 1/2 cups cold water

Method : 1. Mix rice with water and steam or boil for 30 minutes. Add sugar and stir well. 2. Grease inside of a 7-inch bowl with a little lard. Place red plums (or other candied fruit) in center of bowl. Then, working outward in circular fashion, arrange green plums, lotus seeds, and raisins. Use dates and chestnuts as you reach edge of bowl. 3. Divide steamed rice into two equal portions. Place one portion over fruit arrangement in bowl to form a concave layer. 4. Fry bean paste (or date paste) with 4 tbsps. lard, stirring constantly to prevent burning. Use all of paste to form layer on top of rice in bowl. Then place remaining portion of rice on top of this to form final layer. 5. Place bowl in steamer and steam pudding for 20 minutes. 6. Boil sauce mixture, stirring constantly until it thickens. 7. Using a spatula to loosen edges, turn steamed pudding out of inverted bowl onto large plate or platter. 8. Pour the hot sauce over pudding before serving.

Note : Sweet bean paste is called *tou sa* in Chinese, *an* in Japanese. It can be purchased already prepared or can be made at home by boiling red beans with sufficient water until they become soft, adding sugar and a little salt, and mashing. Red date paste is made by boiling dried dates until soft, removing skins and seeds, and mashing. One small can of drained fruit cocktail may be substituted for the dried fruit and nuts listed above. Syrup from fruit cocktail may be substituted for part of water in making sauce for pudding.

Desserts

163

Honeyed Apples

Ingredients:

2 apples (1/2 lb.)	Oil for deep-frying
2 egg whites, unbeaten	3 tbsps. oil
2 tbsps. cornstarch	10 tbsps. sugar
2 tbsps. flour	1 tbsp. sesame seeds

Method: Pare and core apples and cut each into 12 pieces. 2. Mix unbeaten egg whites, cornstarch, and flour to form batter. 3. Add apples to batter and mix well until each piece is coated. 4. Heat deep-fry oil and fry coated apple pieces until they turn light brown. Remove from oil and drain. 5. Heat 3 tbsps. oil, add sugar, and stir constantly until sugar melts. 6. Add apples and sesame seed and stir until apples are coated with syrup. 7. Place apples on greased dish and serve hot with a bowl of cold water on the side. Pick up apples with chopsticks or tongs and dip in cold water before eating.

Note: Bananas may be prepared in the same way.

Fried Custard

Ingredients:

A	B
3 egg yolks	Oil for deep-frying
1 cup cold water	3 tbsps. cornstarch
1/2 cup flour	3 tbsps. sesame seeds, toasted and
1 tbsp. cornstarch	ground
1 tbsp. sugar	3 tbsps. sugar
1 tsp. almond extract, or 2 tsps. sesame powder	

Method: 1. Mix A ingredients thoroughly and cook, stirring constantly until mixture becomes firm. 2. Remove mixture to a flat dish to cool. 3. After it has cooled, cut into strips and sprinkle with 3 tbsps. cornstarch. 4. Heat oil and deep-fry strips until they become golden brown. 5. Mix sesame seeds and sugar, sprinkle fried strips with mixture, and serve hot.

Fried Sweet Potato Balls

Ingredients:

1 lb. sweet potatoes	6 tbsps. water
8 tbsps. sugar	1 cup white sesame seeds
1 egg	Oil for deep-frying
2 tbsps. flour	

Method: 1. Steam sweet potatoes until very soft. Mash or strain through a sieve. 2. When cool, mix with sugar and egg. 3. Form small balls, using a tablespoon. 4. Mix flour and water, coat sweet potato balls with mixture, and roll them in sesame seeds. 5. Fry sweet potato balls in deep oil.

Glazed Sweet Potatoes

Ingredients :
1 lb. sweet potatoes
8 tbsps. sugar
1 tbsp. oil
Oil for deep-frying

Method : Peel sweet potatoes and cut into pieces about French-fry size.
2. Fry potatoes in deep oil until golden brown. Remove to a plate. 3.
Heat 1 tbsp. oil in pan over low flame (to avoid burning), add sugar, and
stir constantly over medium flame until sugar is melted. 4. Cook about
2 minutes more until sugar forms a thick syrup. 5. Dip fried sweet potatoes
into syrup until they are well coated. Syrup should form threads as you
remove potatoes from it. Serve potatoes hot.

Almond Jelly with Mixed Fruits

Ingredients :

3 sheets gelatin (or 2 pkgs. Knox
  gelatin or equivalent
  amount agar agar)
5 cups water

4 oz. (6 tbsps.) condensed milk,
  sweetened to taste
2 tsps. almond extract
1 can fruit cocktail (including
  syrup)

Method : 1. Dissolve gelatin in 5 cups water and bring to boil. Strain liquid
through muslin cloth. 2. Add condensed milk and almond extract and stir
well. 3. Pour into flat dish and allow to set. Cool in refrigerator. 4.
Before serving, cut into diamond-shaped pieces and mix with fruit cocktail.

Fried Cookies

Ingredients:

2 cups flour
1 tbsp. lard or Crisco
1/2 cup sugar
3 tbsps. water (more or less, according to quality of flour)

1 tbsp. sesame seed (sautéed in an ungreased pan)
Oil for deep-frying

Method: 1. Knead dough with all above ingredients except oil. 2. Roll dough out and cut into strips 2 inches long and 1 inch wide. 3. Make a slit lengthwise in center of each strip and bring one end of strip through slit to form a twist. Use flour as needed in making these twists, but not too much or the dough will become tough. 4. Deep-fry cookies to light brown.

Note: See color photo facing page 158.

Almond Cookies

Ingredients:

1 1/2 cups flour
1 tsp. salt
1/2 tsp. soda
6 tbsps. lard or other shortening
1/2 tsp. almond extract

1 egg
1/4 cup large-crystal sugar
10 blanched almonds
1 egg yolk, beaten with 1 tbsp. water

Method: Blanch almonds and remove skins. 2. Combine all ingredients except almonds and egg yolk-water mixture. Knead into a soft dough. 3. Divide dough into 10 portions and shape each into a flat cookie. 4. Brush top of each cookie with mixture of beaten egg yolk and water. 5. Press a blanched almond into center of each cookie. 6. Bake in moderate oven for about 10 minutes until light brown in color.

Walnut Tea

Ingredients:

2 cups shelled walnuts
1/2 cup uncooked rice, soaked in water overnight

6 Chinese red dates, boiled, skinned, and seeded
2 cups sugar
7 cups water

Method: 1. Blanch walnuts in boiling water for 10 minutes and remove skins. 2. Grind walnuts, rice, and dates together in a mortar, mixer, or Japanese *suribachi,* adding 1 cup water a little at a time while grinding, so that result will be a paste. 3. Add 3 cups water to paste, mix well, and squeeze out liquid through a muslin bag. 4. Add remaining 3 cups water and 2 cups sugar to this liquid and cook in deep saucepan for 10 minutes, stirring constantly. 5. Serve hot in teacups.

Note: Rice flour may be substituted in equivalent amount for rice. Dates may be omitted.

Full Moon Dumplings

Ingredients :

1/4 lb. sesame seed

1/2 lb. lard or other solid shortening (or hard fat)

1/2 lb. sugar

4 cups glutinous rice flour

Method : 1. Wash sesame seed. While it is still wet, toast it in a frying pan without oil. This must be done carefully, since sesame seed burns very easily. 2. Grind toasted sesame seed. 3. Combine sugar and ground sesame seed with lard and roll into small balls the size of cherries. Allow balls to harden on a plate. 4. Add sufficient water to glutinous flour to form a dough. Knead dough well and roll it into round pieces about 1 1/2 inches in diameter. 5. Place one of sesame seed balls in center of each round of dough and fold dough over to form dumplings. 6. Drop dumplings in boiling water, stirring constantly until they rise to the top. Let them cook for several minutes. Serve hot in water used for boiling.

Note : These dumplings are traditionally eaten by the Chinese on the day of the first full moon in January. The dumplings symbolize "fullness" or "entirety." There are various kinds, since different fillings may be used. Among these fillings, in addition to sesame seed, are walnuts, dried fruits, and sweet bean paste.

Desserts

167

SUGGESTED MENUS

LUNCHEON

(for four persons)
Fried Noodles (page 140)
Velvet Chicken and Sweet Corn Soup (page 150)

(for four persons)
Meat and Vegetable Buns (page 132)
Hot Tea (page 14)

(for four persons)
Noodles in Broth (page 139)
Fried Cookies (page 166)

(for four persons)
Scrambled Eggs with Shredded Pork (page 98)
Chilled Cucumbers and Red Radishes (page 121)
Boiled Rice (page 14)
Tomato Soup with Egg Flower (page 152)

DINNER

(for six persons)
Crisp Roasted Duck (page 37)
Egg Roll (page 97)
Fried Beef with Celery (page 72)
Stewed Meat Balls with Cabbage (page 91)
Velvet Chicken and Sweet Corn Soup (page 150)
Chinese Bread (page 144)

(for six to eight persons)
Sweet and Sour Fish (page 46)
Empress Chicken (page 27)
Egg Fu Yung (page 100)
Creamed Chinese Cabbage (page 117)
Spring Rolls (page 131)

Beef Soup with Quail Eggs (page 152)

(for six to eight persons)
Sweet and Sour Pork (page 86)
Fried Chicken with Walnuts (page 34)
Fried Beef with Green Peppers (page 74)
Meat and Vegetable Salad (page 122)
Shredded Meat and Vegetable Soup (page 153)

(for eight to ten persons)
Smoked Fish (page 48)
Boiled Eggs with Soy Sauce (page 103)
Sliced Cold Chicken (page 36)
Chilled Sweet and Sour Cucumbers (page 120)
Fried Chicken Fillet with Peanuts (page 33)
Fried Shrimp Balls (page 55)
Braised Shark's Fins (page 66)
Egg Roll (page 97)
Fried Mixed Vegetables (page 112)
Braised Pork with Eggs (page 89)
Abalone Soup with Meat Balls (page 158)
Boiled Rice (page 14)
Almond Jelly with Mixed Fruits (page 165)
Hot Tea (page 14)

FOODSTUFFS

Abalone, *Pao yü:* 鮑魚
Almonds, *Hsing jên:* 杏仁
Aniseed, *Pa chiao:* 八角
Apple, *P'ing kuo:* 萍果
Asparagus, *Lung hsu ts'ai:* 龍鬚菜

Bamboo shoot, *Tung sun:* 冬笋
Bean curd, *Tou fu:* 豆腐
Bean curd sheets, *Tou fu yu:* 豆腐衣
Bean paste, sweet, *Tou sa:* 豆沙
Bean sprouts, *Tou ya ts'ai:* 豆芽菜
Beans, green, *Lü tou:* 緑豆
Beef, *Niu jou:* 牛肉
Birds' nests, *Yen wou:* 燕窩

Cabbage, Chinese, *Pai ts'ai:* 白菜
Cabbage, round, *Yang pai ts'ai:* 洋白菜
Carp, *Li yü:* 鯉魚
Carrots, *Hu lo po:* 胡蘿蔔
Catsup (tomato), *Fan ch'ieh chiang:* 蕃茄醬
Cauliflower, *Ts'ai hua:* 菜花
Celery, *Ch'in ts'ai:* 芹菜
Chestnuts, *Li tzŭ:* 栗子
Chicken, *Chi jou:* 鶏肉
Chili peppers, *La chiao:* 辣椒
Clams, *Ko li:* 蛤蜊
Corn (sweet), *Yü mi:* 玉米
Cornstarch, *Lin fên:* 菱粉
Crab, *P'ang hsieh:* 螃蟹
Cucumber, *Huang kua:* 黄瓜
Cuttlefish, *You yü:* 魷魚

Dates, honey, *Mi tsao:* 密棗
Dates, red, *Hung tsao:* 紅棗
Duck, *Ya tzŭ:* 鴨子
Dumplings, *Chiao tzŭ:* 餃子

Eggplant, *Ch'ieh tzŭ:* 茄子
Eggs, chicken, *Chi tan:* 鶏蛋
Eggs, quail, *An ch'un tan:* 鵪鶉蛋

Fish, *Yü:* 魚
Flour, rice, *Mi fên:* 米粉
Flour, wheat, *Mien fên:* 麵粉

Garlic, *Suan:* 蒜
Giblets (chicken), *Chi chen kan:* 鶏胗肝
Ginger, *Chiang:* 薑

Ham, *Huo t'ui:* 火腿
Honey, *Fen mi:* 蜂蜜

Jellyfish, *Hai chê:* 海蜇

Kidney, pork, *Chu yao:* 猪腰

Lard, *Chu yu:* 猪油
Leek, *Ts'ung:* 葱
Lettuce, *Shêng ts'ai:* 生菜
Lima beans, *Ts'an tou:* 蚕豆
Liver, beef, *Niu kan:* 牛肝
Liver, chicken, *Chi kan:* 鶏肝
Lotus leaves, *Ho yeh:* 荷葉
Lotus root, *Ou:* 藕
Lotus seeds, *Lien tzŭ:* 蓮子

Melon, white gourd, *Tung kua:* 冬瓜

Monosodium glutamate, *Wei ching:* 味精
Mushrooms, dried, *Tung ku:* 冬菇
Mustard, *Chieh mo:* 芥末
Mustard greens, *Chieh lan ts'ai:* 芥蘭菜

Noodles, *Mien tiao:* 麵條

Oil, chicken, *Chi yu:* 鶏油
Oil, peanut, *Hua shêng yu:* 花生油
Oil, red pepper, *La yu:* 辣油
Oil, sesame, *Ma yu:* 麻油
Oil, soy bean, *Tou yu:* 豆油
Onion, *Yang ts'ung:* 洋葱
Oysters, *Li huang:* 蜊蟥

Peanuts, *Lê hua shêng:* 落花生
Peas, green, *Wan tou:* 菀豆
Pepper, black, *Hua chiao:* 花椒
Pepper, chili, *La chiao:* 辣椒
Pepper, green, *Ch'ing chiao:* 青椒
Pepper, red (ground), *Hung la chiao:* 紅辣椒
Pigeon, *Kê tzǔ:* 鴿子
Pineapple, *Po lo:* 菠羅
Plums, green, *Ch'ing mei:* 青梅
Plums, red, *Hung mei:* 紅梅
Pork, *Chu jou:* 猪肉
Potatoes, *Yang shan yü:* 洋山芋
Prawns, *Ming hsia:* 明蝦
Pumpkin, *Nan kua:* 南瓜

Radishes, red, *Hung lo po:* 紅蘿蔔
Ravioli, *Hun t'ung:* 餛飩
Rice, cooked, *Fan:* 飯
Rice, glutinous, *Nou mi:* 糯米

Rice, uncooked, *Ta mi:* 大米
Salt, *Yen:* 塩
Scallops, *Kan pei:* 干貝
Sea cucumber, *Hai shen:* 海參
Sesame oil, *Ma yu:* 麻油
Sesame paste, *Chih ma chiang:* 芝麻醬
Sesame seeds, *Chih ma:* 芝麻
Shark's fins, *Yü ch'ih:* 魚翅
Shrimp, *Hsia jên:* 蝦仁
Snow peas, *Wan tou cha:* 豌豆莢
Soy bean paste, *Chiang:* 醬
Soy beans, green, *Mou tou:* 毛豆
Soy beans, dried, *Ta tou:* 大豆
Soy sauce, *Chiang yu:* 醬油
Spinach, *Po ts'ai:* 菠菜
Spring onions, *Jei ts'ai:* 韮菜
String beans, *Pien tou:* 扁豆
Sugar, brown, *Hung t'ang:* 紅糖
Sugar, granulated, *Sa t'ang:* 砂糖
Sugar, white, *Pai t'ang:* 白糖
Sweet potatoes, *Pai shu:* 白薯

Tea, *Ch'a:* 茶
Tomatoes, *Fan ch'ieh:* 蕃茄
Turkey, *Huo chi:* 火鶏
Turnips, *Ta lo po:* 大蘿蔔

Vermicelli (green bean type), *Fên ssǔ:* 粉絲
Vermicelli (seaweed type), *Yang fên:* 洋粉
Vinegar, *Ts'u:* 醋

Walnuts, *Ho t'ao:* 核桃
Water chestnuts, *Po chi:* 荸薺
Wine, Chinese, *Chiu:* 酒

INDEX